HERE

LIVED

THE

CALIFORNIANS

Books by Oscar Lewis

BONANZA INN (with Carroll D. Hall)

I REMEMBER CHRISTINE (a novel)

THE UNCERTAIN JOURNEY (a novel)

SILVER KINGS

SEA ROUTES TO THE GOLD FIELDS

CALIFORNIA HERITAGE

THE LOST YEARS (a fantasy)

SAGEBRUSH CASINOS

HAWAII, GEM OF THE PACIFIC

THE TOWN THAT DIED LAUGHING

HIGH SIERRA COUNTRY

BAY WINDOW BOHEMIA

HERE LIVED THE CALIFORNIANS

Old Whaling Station, Monterey. Standing at 391 Decatur Street, this handsome adobe, with characteristic second-floor balcony across its front, was built in 1855 and was long the headquarters of the Portuguese whaling ships then operating in North Pacific waters.   *Photograph by Lee Blaisdell, Monterey*

HERE

LIVED

THE

CALIFORNIANS

BY OSCAR LEWIS

RINEHART & COMPANY, INC.

NEW YORK   TORONTO

Published simultaneously in Canada by
Clarke, Irwin & Company, Ltd., Toronto

© 1957 by Oscar Lewis
Manufactured in the United States of America
Library of Congress Catalog Card Number: 57–5058

CONTENTS

LIST OF ILLUSTRATIONS

LIST OF ILLUSTRATIONS

Following page

PART FIVE:

LIST OF ILLUSTRATIONS

FOREWORD

A wise man once stated that in order to learn the history of any country one need but examine the houses in which its inhabitants, past and present, have lived. An ingenious theory this, and by no means as far-fetched as it might at first appear, though it must be granted that this method of reading history calls for an observant eye and a logical mind on the part of the student. One possessed of these qualities can, however, go a long way toward determining the way of life of a people, their characteristics, customs, and degree of culture, on no other evidence than that presented by their domestic arrangements, including the houses in which they lived.

To one interested in testing the validity of that hypothesis, California should prove a particularly inviting field. For during the comparatively brief time that has passed since the first permanent settlements were established there — a period of less than two centuries — the region has passed through a succession of phases that, for number and variety, cannot be matched elsewhere in the nation. Moreover, there exist today a goodly number of buildings dating from each period of California's brief but eventful history. These range all the way from the still-existing stone shelters of certain of the aboriginal tribes to the glass-and-chrome creations of the more advanced of the region's modern designers.

In planning this over-all survey of the sorts of houses Californians have chosen to live in from earliest times to the present, certain problems have presented themselves, particularly as regards the arrangement of the material. The final decision has been to group the various structures described and pictured, not by localities, but by the historical periods to which they belong. This seems the more logical arrangement, and for the convenience of those looking for houses in particular areas, the map facing page 3 has been provided.

The chapters into which the material has been gathered are arranged chronologically, beginning with the thick-walled adobes put up by the earliest Spanish and Mexican settlers, followed by the frame dwellings of the pioneer Yankee and other foreign residents of the province, then by surviving examples of Gold Rush architecture, and so on down to recent times.

By adopting this manner of presentation, certain facts become clear, facts that tend to bear out the theory advanced above. One is that the types of residences the Californians built at different periods of the region's history were in the main determined, not by the personal preferences of their owners, but by the standards in vogue at the time. In other words domestic architecture, here as elsewhere, followed the trends of the times, each phase of California's history having a clearly defined style, whether it be the adobes of the Spanish and Mexican periods, the austere frame cottages of Gold Rush days, or any one of the series of phases that followed. The main difference is that in California these phases were more numerous, and followed one another more rapidly, than in most other parts of the country.

The state is fortunate in that, of the structures put up in the earliest period, a comparatively large number still stand, not only the old missions themselves but a variety of others: town halls, custom houses, soldiers' barracks and other types of official buildings, stables, inns and barrooms, and — of particular interests to us here — the residences of pioneer settlers both in the towns and on the big outlying ranches.

That so many of these picturesque adobes have survived can be ascribed mainly to the fact that those who put them up built sturdily and well. Their thick walls were well designed to withstand the wear and tear of the years, provided only that the earthen bricks of which they were composed were shielded from exposure to the weather. This last was accomplished both by a coating of plaster on their outer surfaces and by a broad overhang on their roofs.

However, when these elements were neglected and winter rains were permitted to reach the walls, their dissolution was speedy, only a few years being needed to reduce once substantial buildings to heaps of rubble. This was the fate of many such structures during the first several decades following the taking over of the province by the Yankees in 1846. As time passed, however, the historic importance of these old buildings came to be recognized, and a widespread demand arose for the restoration and preservation of those still standing.

Thus from the early years of the present century down to the present a great deal has been accomplished, both by the state itself and by a number of historic-minded organizations of a semiofficial character. Through their efforts, many such buildings have been acquired, restored, and permanently preserved for the benefit of present and future generations. In addition to such activities, over the years numerous individuals, recognizing the charm of the adobes, have purchased them for use as dwellings. These have in the main been careful to see that in the process of modernization the old-world character of the houses was not destroyed.

Much the same procedure has been followed, though on a smaller scale, with houses dating from other periods of the state's beginnings, particularly with those belonging to the Gold Rush era. The fact that the number of such structures that have been singled out for preservation is far fewer than the earlier adobes does not mean that the Gold Rush is regarded as a less important or picturesque period than that of the padres and rancheros, but merely that their houses disappeared far more rapidly than had the others.

The reasons why this last was so are obvious. In the first place most residents of the gold towns expected their stays there to be brief; consequently, their living quarters were usually makeshift affairs that had been hastily thrown up and which their owners, upon moving elsewhere, felt no hesitation about abandoning. Furthermore, by the mid-1850s, the populations of most of the Mother Lode settlements had declined drastically, with many of their buildings standing vacant, doomed either to fall into ruin or to be torn down and their materials used elsewhere.

During the century that has passed since the Gold Rush drew to a close, domestic architecture in California has progressed through a series of more or less clearly defined stages. The first of these, covering the decade from 1855 to the close of the Civil War, saw many changes in the economy of the new state, with what had been virtually its only industry — placer mining — being first supplemented, and then all but supplanted, by a variety of others.

One of the most important of these changes was the rise of agriculture, for this included not only the founding of huge wheat ranches throughout the Sacramento and San Joaquin valleys, but the setting out of orchards and vineyards at many points along the coast and the beginnings of diversified farming in those areas. At the same time other enterprises were being launched throughout the length and breadth of the state; quartz and hydraulic mining on the western slopes of the Sierra, lumbering in the extensive redwood and pine forests on the north coast and inland, and the running of ever larger herds of cattle and sheep on the limitless ranges of the south.

Nor was that all. For along with the rise of these industries sprang up a variety of other activities, all closely related to those mentioned and in the main necessary to their efficient functioning. These included not only banks and other houses for the financing of such enterprises, and brokerage firms for the handling of their products, but mills to process what they produced, railroads, steamers, and other vessels to carry them to the world's markets and bring back needed supplies and equipment, and much else. In short, what a few years earlier had been a simple frontier economy had become something far more complex, ushering in an entirely new phase in the development of the state.

Of the California residences dating from that transition period, a number of excellent examples remain, although the majority have long since disappeared, victims either of the passage of the years or, if located in the cities, of falling before the hands of the wreckers.

Among the most interesting of the surviving buildings of that period are the farmhouses, particularly those put up on the wheat ranches of the central valley during the 1860s, 1870s, and later. For the enterprises of which their owners were the heads were by no means small, the ranches often having an area of 20,000 acres or more, with employees during the planting and harvesting seasons numbering into the hundreds, and in general the proprietors lived on a scale no less magnificent. Hence, some of the valley ranch houses during the heyday of the wheat period were truly impressive examples of mid-Victorian opulence: sprawling, two-story frame structures containing a score or more of rooms, their spacious downstairs chambers fitted up with elegance and their exteriors complex masses of towers, turrets, and gables in the best style of the day.

It was an ostentatious age, and, the fast-expanding economy of the region having put certain enterprisers in possession of large fortunes, these proceeded to build residences in keeping with their newly acquired wealth and position. Thus throughout the 1870s and later, there arose on Nob Hill in San Francisco, on the oak-studded meadows to the south of that city, at Sacramento, Santa Barbara, Los Angeles, and elsewhere, a group of mansions that for size and complexity surpassed any the state had previously seen. By far the greater number of these have likewise long since passed from view, and all but a few of those now living know of their wonders only at second hand, either through the recollections of oldsters, or from descriptions — illustrated by woodcuts — to be found on the yellowing pages of certain local newspapers or weekly magazines. Fortunately, however, a few examples have survived the hazards of the years, and of these a number have been described and pictured on the pages that follow.

Later phases of the evolution of California domestic architecture are covered in the final chapters, including certain typical examples of the scores of pretentious residences put up in various parts of the state during the early 1900s.

Acknowledgment of help received from various sources during the compiling of this work will be found at the end of the book.

HERE

LIVED

THE

CALIFORNIANS

Weaverville

Redding

Red Bluff

Chico

SACRAMENTO R.

Cloverdale

Nevada City
Grass Valley
Marysville   Dutch Flat

Fort Ross
SONOMA   Napa
          St. Helena   Georgetown
Santa Rosa
   Glen Ellen
     Sonoma   Sacramento
Petaluma
                    Volcano

San Francisco   Martinez
              Oakland
San Mateo   CONTRA COSTA
Burlingame   Belmont   Stockton
 Atherton   Menlo Park
           San Jose

         Saratoga

SAN JOAQUIN R.

           Mariposa

       San Juan
        Bautista

Monterey

San Simeon

SAN LUIS OBISPO

     San Luis Obispo

California

Miles

0   50   100

DEATH VALLEY

MOJAVE DESERT

Santa Barbara
   Montecito

      VENTURA

      San Fernando
Glendale   Pasadena
          San Marino
Los Angeles   San Gabriel
           Whittier
Wilmington   Anaheim
       Long Beach

                San Juan Capistrano

SANTA
CATALINA I.

Pacific Ocean

palacios

San Diego

PART

I

SPANISH AND MEXICAN ADOBES

From earliest times down to the present, domestic architecture in California has passed through a series of clearly defined phases, each reflecting not only such elements of the environment as climate, the types of building materials readily at hand, and so on, but also — and equally — the cultural backgrounds of those residents who were in the majority during different periods of the region's evolution.

The California Indians, long the sole inhabitants of its mountains, plains, and coastal valleys, were by nature a nomadic people, moving from place to place as they sought new hunting grounds or followed the seasons in quest of favorite foods: wild berries, grapes, and certain varieties of water lilies throughout the spring and summer, acorns on the oak-studded valleys and foothills in the fall, and the like. The consequence was that the aboriginals of California possessed few permanent habitations, their shelters in the main consisting of the skins of deer or other animals stretched over poles, which could be easily dismantled and, together with their other meager belongings, transported to a new site. The mild climate prevailing over most of the region was a factor, too, in this informal manner of life, for with the coming of winter cold in the more northern areas, the natives had but to make their way down to the balmy valleys that lay farther to the south.

Not until the arrival, in the second half of the eighteenth century, of the first parties of Spanish soldiers and priests from Mexico, and the laying out of permanent settlements in the new land, did California enter the second phase of its evolution from primitive wilderness to complex and populous modern state. Beginning in 1769, the new-comers founded a series of missions, pueblos, and presidios at points along the coast from San Diego northward to San Francisco and beyond. The buildings they proceeded to put up — the mission churches and soldiers' quarters alike — conformed both in appearance and in the materials used to the architecture of their mother country, Spain. Thus was ushered in what has been termed the Age of the Adobe, a period that was destined to last well over three quarters of a century.

Scores of structures belonging to that era still stand, not only in the coastal area from San Francisco Bay southward to the Mexican border, but in the interior valleys and even in certain of the old mining towns in the Sierra foothills. They range in size and design from the more impressive of the old missions — among them those at Carmel, Santa Barbara, and San Gabriel — to tiny, one-room ranch houses. All, however, have one thing in common: their thick, sturdy walls are composed of adobe bricks.

The all but universal use of adobe as a building material through-out that period sprang from a variety of circumstances. First, it was a type of construction with which the friars and military authorities of the province were thoroughly familiar, as it had long been widely used both in Spain and Mexico. Second, the climate of the southern half of the region, a land of long, dry summers where little rain fell at any season of the year, made that type of building both practicable and, if

4

properly cared for, long lasting. Finally, and of at least equal importance, was the fact that not only was the material used in the making of the bricks close at hand, but their manufacture was so simple a process that the native Indians had little difficulty mastering the art.

The adobes put up during that period were of two general types. By the earliest and most widely used method, the heavy black soil or clay of the region was mixed with grass, twigs, or other binding material and formed into bricks which were dried in the sun. These were then laid one upon the other, with a thin layer of mud between each row, to form the wall, and the whole was covered on the outside with a coating of plaster to protect it from the elements. The second process — of which a few examples still exist, mostly in the towns at the southern end of the Mother Lode — consisted of employing building forms similar to those used in present-day concrete construction. The walls were made by filling the space between the forms with dampened earth, tamping it down solidly and, after the forms were removed, applying a protective coating to the outer surface.

The more pretentious adobes, not only the mission buildings and the official structures put up in the presidios — or military posts — and towns, but the private dwellings both in the settlements and on the outlying ranches, often had roofs of red tiles. These were supported by sturdy, hand-hewn timbers fashioned from the trunks of trees growing nearby. The timbers were bound together with cowhide thongs, since no nails were available in the province during that early period.

As their builders were well aware, these buildings would last indefinitely, provided certain precautionary rules were observed. One was that, as stated, the earthen walls be protected from the elements by an outer coating of a water-resistant substance, commonly a thin layer of sand with which lime was mixed. After the walls had been coated, they were whitewashed. Moreover, it was desirable that the roof be kept in repair and that the eaves project far enough beyond the building so that the bulk of the rain water fell clear of the walls.

When one or another of these measures was neglected for any considerable period of time, winter rains reduced the adobe bricks to mud, and the entire structure gradually fell into ruin. That was the fate of hundreds of such buildings, ranging from modest ranch houses to large public and privately owned structures all over the southern and central parts of the state. However, a goodly number still stand, and these in nearly every instance are carefully preserved today, either by their individual owners, or by their having been designated historical monuments and taken into the state park system. In either case, there is every likelihood of their remaining for the benefit of present and future generations of Californians, picturesque relics of a long-vanished era in the history of their state. On the following pages are described and pictured a representative group of these early-day structures.

Some three miles to the east of Petaluma, atop a knoll overlooking the broad, hill-rimmed Santa Rosa Valley, stands the Casa Grande, northern California's largest adobe building, which in the period just prior to the American Conquest was one of the showplaces of the Mexican province's northern frontier.

Begun in 1834, the same year its owner, General Mariano Guadalupe Vallejo, acquired title to his big Petaluma rancho — an area covering some 75,000 acres — it was intended to serve two purposes. These were: First, to be a headquarters and rallying point for those settlers Vallejo and the Mexican authorities at Monterey hoped to attract to the fertile farming and grazing lands north of San Francisco Bay, and — second, and at least equally important — to check further penetration into the province by the Russians, who more than two decades earlier had established themselves at Fort Ross, a scant forty miles to the northwest.

Vallejo was a man of large ideas, with more than a touch of the grandiose in his nature, and when he set out to build his Petaluma casa nothing would do but that it must exceed in size and impressiveness any other man-made structure within a radius of many miles. That

6

1. Casa Grande, Petaluma. This, the largest adobe structure to be built in northern California, was erected by General Mariano Vallejo in 1833-34, largely by Indian labor, to serve as headquarters of his huge Rancho Petaluma, comprising some 75,000 acres. Long unoccupied, it has recently been taken over by the state of California and is being carefully restored to its original condition. *Photograph from Duncan H. Olmsted, Petaluma*

ambition was fully realized. Even today the Old Adobe, as it is known throughout the region, is an impressive sight, and this despite the fact that one entire wing was destroyed by a fire and that the remainder of the edifice has suffered from many years of neglect and vandalism.

While its builder and owner, a man of many interests, lived there for only brief periods, spending most of his time at a second home near the Sonoma Mission, some twelve miles distant, the Petaluma casa was the scene of great activity during its heyday. Not only was it frequently used to house those of Vallejo's guests who could not be put up at his Sonoma establishment, but there were centered the many enterprises incident to the development and operation of his Petaluma rancho.

In this last-named capacity, it sheltered a company of soldiers charged with holding in check the warlike Indians of the area, while at the same time numerous groups of natives — numbering, it is said, as many as 600 — were stationed there. These included not only those who planted the surrounding fields to wheat and other crops and the vaqueros who watched over Vallejo's cattle, but artisans engaged in milling, weaving, leather-tanning, soapmaking, carpentry, and other crafts.

The big, two-story casa was laid out in the form of a U, enclosing an inner patio where each morning squads of workers, under the charge of their overseers, were assembled for roll call before being assigned to their tasks of the day. Built of adobe bricks, its walls four feet thick at their base, and with inner partitions, roof, and broad outside galleries of heavy, hand-hewn timbers bound together by rawhide thongs, the structure had a solidity that has enabled it to survive more than a century of neglect.

From time to time movements have been launched for its restoration, either by means of funds raised by private subscription, or by having it designated a California historic landmark, in which case it would come under the protection and care of the state itself. Fortu-

2. Blue Wing Inn, Sonoma. One of the most celebrated of
California hostelries dating from Spanish and Mexican days is
this thick-walled adobe structure, which stands on Spain Street,
directly opposite the northernmost of the chain of early missions. Throughout the 1840s and later it was a popular stopping place for those traveling between San Francisco Bay
settlements and the upper Sacramento Valley. *Photograph
by Edgar Waite, Sonoma*

nately, this campaign has borne fruit, for recently a comprehensive program of restoration got under way, one that assures its preservation.

The town of Sonoma, where the last and northernmost of the early missions, that of San Francisco de Solano, was founded in 1824, is rich in buildings dating from the period prior to the taking over of the province by the Yankees. In the northeast corner of its central plaza stands the mission itself, a low, tile-roofed adobe which, after having long been used as a storehouse by early-day American ranchers and fallen into semiruin, was restored to a semblance of its original condition in the early 1900s. Today it is a state museum, housing relics of pioneer days and examples of the baskets, arrows, and other handiwork of the Indian tribes that once inhabited the area.

Nearby stands the Blue Wing Inn, an adobe put up in 1840 and reputed to be the first hostelry north of San Francisco Bay; it was a popular gathering place for visitors to that outpost settlement both before and after the American Conquest. Another historic structure facing the plaza is the Sonoma Barracks, built in 1836 to house the Mexican soldiers charged with patrolling the province's northern frontier. This, a two-story adobe with a second-floor balcony across its front, was taken over as a headquarters by the band of American settlers who in the summer of 1846 captured the town and set up the short-lived Bear Flag Republic.

Other old houses facing the plaza or adjacent to it include the El Dorado Hotel, originally a single-story adobe building which during the years just before and after the Americans took over was a popular stopping place for visitors to the town. Later its capacity was doubled by the addition of a wooden second story, plus an upstairs balcony. Next door to the Sonoma Barracks stands the old Vallejo home, where the doughty general lived during the early days of the settlement and from which he directed the affairs of his huge domain. The lofty tower that once surmounted the building, to which Vallejo would climb, spyglass in hand, to watch over his grazing herds, has long since disappeared. Nearby, on the northern side of the plaza, is the home of Vallejo's brother Salvador and, at the southwest corner, that of his brother-in-law, Jacob P. Leese.

Some five years after the taking over of the province by the United States, Vallejo moved into his new and grander house, to which he gave the romantic name, Lachryma Montis, meaning "tears of the mountain," supposedly because of a mountain spring on its grounds. This stands at the northern end of the town, surrounded by a grove of wide-spreading trees, and is now preserved as a state historical monument. Built in the ornate, begabled style fancied by prosperous Californians during the 1850s and later, it contains ten rooms, in which have been assembled a collection of furniture and household ornaments dating from that period. Nearby is a second structure patterned after a Swiss chalet; the bricks and hand-hewn timbers which were used in its construction are said to have been brought round the Horn. This is now known as the Vallejo Museum. In it are displayed clothing, jewelry, and other memorabilia that once belonged to the general and his lady.

Some twenty-five miles to the southeast of Sonoma, in the wooded Alhambra Valley near the point where it has its outlet on the shores of upper San Francisco Bay, stands a picturesque adobe ranch house which is still in excellent condition for all its venerable age. Built in the mid-40s of the last century, the sturdy, two-story structure was long the home of Vicente José Ramon Martinez, younger son of Ignacio Martinez who, after serving as commandante of the San Francisco Presidio during the late 1820s and early 1830s, settled on his big Rancho El Pinole in 1836. Vicente built his adobe, not on his father's ranch but on land close by, and there remained for the balance of his life, running herds of cattle over the surrounding hills and in his spacious ranch house entertaining neighbors and visitors who passed that way with the open-handed hospitality characteristic of the period. Following Vicente's death, the house and surrounding property became

3. Lachryma Montis, Sonoma. Picturesquely situated at the edge of the town of Sonoma is this commodious Victorian residence, long the home of General Mariano Vallejo. Standing in the midst of a 17-acre state park, its grounds are ornamented by quaint cast-iron statues characteristic of the 1850s. *Photograph by Harry W. Abrahams, San Francisco*

4. Vallejo's Swiss Chalet, Sonoma. Standing on the grounds of General Vallejo's Sonoma estate, Lachryma Montis, this quaint structure, having the second-story overhang characteristic of Swiss domestic architecture, was built in 1850. The bricks that compose its outer walls are said to have been brought out as ballast in the holds of early-day sailing ships. *Photograph by Edgar Waite, Sonoma*

5. Vicente Martinez House, Martinez. In the Alhambra Valley a short distance from the present town of Martinez stands this typical early California ranch house, with a broad balcony across its front onto which doors open from both the ground floor and second-story rooms. It was built by a son of Ignacio Martinez, commandante of the San Francisco Presidio from 1828 to 1831. *Photograph by Hammond Studio, Martinez*

a part of the ranch of John Strentzel, father-in-law of the naturalist, John Muir, whose bay-windowed Victorian residence, described in a later chapter, stands not far distant.

In the presidio of San Francisco is to be seen a low, tile-roofed structure with massive walls and deeply recessed windows that has the distinction of being the first building to be erected on the site of the future city. It is now known as the Officers' Club, and its original outlines have been changed by later additions. The building dates from the year 1776 when a party of Spanish soldiers under the command of Lieutenant José Joaquin Moraga arrived from the south, charged with establishing a military post on the shores of the then remote bay.

Moraga chose a site on a sage-covered hillside just within the Golden Gate, and his men, together with members of the crew of the barque *San Carlos*, which had meantime arrived at the harbor, set about putting up a group of buildings: a house for the commandante, a chapel, a storeroom, and a number of crude shelters for the soldiers. Work continued throughout the summer and on September 17 of that year the spot was dedicated with, in the words of Father Palóu, who was present, "all the splendor that the place permitted."

Among these "splendors" were the saying of mass in the little chapel, the ringing of bells, and the firing of cannons and muskets both ashore and aboard the *San Carlos*, the sound of which, wrote Father Palóu, "doubtless terrified the heathen, for they did not allow themselves to be seen for days."

Although the military post thus established continued to be maintained throughout the seventy years the Spanish and Mexican flags flew over the province, during most of that period only a squad or two of soldiers were stationed there. Moreover, discipline was lamentably lax, and later visitors to the spot found the grounds uncared for and the buildings in a deplorable condition. When the Americans took over in 1846, few of the structures remained standing and the only weapons visible were several brass cannon, the inscriptions on which

6. Officers' Club, San Francisco. The first building to be erected on the site of San Francisco is this quaint structure, which stands on the grounds of the Presidio and now serves as an Officers' Club. Much changed in appearance by later additions, the original adobe was built in 1776 to be used as the headquarters of Lieutenant José Joaquin Moraga, then in command of the Spanish forces stationed at this northern outpost.   *Photograph by Fred Lyon, Sausalito*

identified them as veterans of Pizarro's conquest of Peru a full three centuries earlier.

Today two of these old firing pieces stand before the entrance of the Officers' Club. The central portion of the club embodies all that remains of the former Spanish presidio — the thick walls of the commandante's house built by Lieutenant Moraga's men in the summer of 1776. Although later additions and restorations have made it difficult to trace the original outlines, the club has a historic interest as the first building to be put up within the confines of the present city, and as such is venerated by all San Franciscans.

Near the northern end of El Camino Real, the old highway that extended from San Diego northward to Sonoma, stands one of the best preserved of the settlements dating from Spanish and Mexican days. This is the village of San Juan Bautista which lies at the southern end of the Santa Clara Valley, an hour's drive to the south of San José and some three miles off the heavily traveled Coast Highway Number 101. As in nearly all other towns of the period, the original buildings are grouped about a central square, the northern side of which is occupied by the Mission San Juan Bautista, one of the largest of the group of such establishments founded by the padres.

Facing the plaza on the west, and side by side with a second old adobe known as the Plaza Hotel, is the Castro House, a handsome, two-story structure, with the low-pitched tile roof, overhanging balcony, and deeply recessed doors and windows characteristic of the more pretentious residences put up by Spanish or Mexican citizens during the late eighteenth and early nineteenth centuries. This was built about 1825 by José de Castro, one of the prominent men of the province and owner of a huge rancho in the area. Following Mexico's independence from Spain in 1822, Castro twice served as acting governor of the province. Later still, at the time of the taking over of California by the United States, he was in command of the Mexican forces in the north, and is credited with having maneuvered the small parties of mounted soldiers under his charge with courage and skill.

17

In 1849, his San Juan casa was sold to one Patrick Breen, member of the ill-fated Donner Party that three years earlier had become snowbound in the Sierra, many of their number perishing before the survivors were rescued the following spring. For a time Breen operated the place as a tavern, and during that period it became a popular overnight stopping place for those traveling between San Francisco and Monterey. For several decades prior to the completion of the coastline railroad connecting those two cities, business at Breen's Tavern was brisk. As many as eleven companies operated stages over the route, and in addition numerous freight wagons passed that way. Stage passengers, together with those traveling on horseback or in their own vehicles, were frequent guests at the inn.

The old adobe, with its massive walls, spacious public rooms downstairs and sleeping quarters above, has, too, its literary associations. For in the early 1880s Helen Hunt Jackson, the transported New Englander then living in California while she studied the plight of the fast-disappearing local Indians, was for a time a guest there, and it was during her stay that she penned the opening chapters of *Ramona*, her widely read novel dealing with that theme. The story is told that the man whom Breen had placed in charge of the premises, on learning that Mrs. Jackson was not a member of the Catholic faith, brusquely ordered her to leave.

The Castro House, along with certain other buildings grouped about the plaza, was taken over some years ago by the state and incorporated into its system of parks. Under the name of the San Juan Bautista State Monument, the whole has been restored and preserved. There each spring a two-day celebration is held, during which residents of the area deck themselves out in the colorful costumes of early Spanish times and perform feats of horsemanship and other amusements popular during "the Days of the Dons."

Standing next door to the Castro House is another of San Juan's historic buildings, the Plaza Hotel, said to have been the first permanent

7. Castro House, San Juan Bautista. One of a group of historically interesting buildings facing the plaza of this quaint town is the two-story adobe shown above, built in 1825 by General José Castro, for a time acting governor of the province and, when the Americans took over in 1846, in command of the Mexican forces in the north. In Gold Rush days it was operated as an inn and was a favorite stopping place for those traveling between Monterey and San Francisco. *Photograph by Sigurd Larsen, San Juan Bautista*

8. Plaza Hotel, San Juan. This, the oldest of San Juan's existing buildings, dates from 1792. Originally a one-story adobe ranch house, in 1856 the second floor and balcony were added and it was converted into a hotel, a rival to the Castro House which stands next door. *Photograph by Sigurd Larsen, San Juan Bautista*

structure put up in the settlement. Originally it was a one-story adobe, its thick walls surmounted by a tile roof. It was built in 1792, five years before work began on the big mission building across the plaza and nearly two decades before the latter was completed.

After serving as a residence for over half a century, it was taken over by an Italian cook named Angelo Zanetta who, in 1856, opened it as a hostelry serving those passing that way over the heavily traveled coast road. Business was evidently good, for two years later Zanetta enlarged the premises by joining it up with another small adobe standing alongside and adding a second story with a balcony across its front, thus converting it into the picturesque hotel to be seen today.

The Plaza, long a regular stopping place for the stages, was highly regarded alike for the quality of the meals served in its dining room and for its well-stocked bar. Still standing in the lobby is the ornate desk where many distinguished guests registered, among them Civil War General William Tecumseh Sherman and the West's colorful cattle king, Henry Miller.

Of particular interest to present-day visitors is the quaint old furniture that has been assembled there, both in the public rooms on the ground floor and in the sleeping quarters upstairs. Fascinating, too, are the time-yellowed posters attached to the bulletin board and displayed on the lobby walls. These include rewards for the apprehension of stage robbers and other desperadoes, timetables of early stage lines that operated over this route, and advertisements of long-vanished health resorts in the neighboring foothills, all redolent of an age and a way of life that have long since passed.

Continuing southward from San Juan Bautista, travelers over the old King's Highway presently reached Monterey, long the most important town in northern California and the capital of the province from 1775 until after the Americans took over in 1846.

Of the existing group of private residences dating from that period, one of the most impressive, and best preserved, is the Casa Amesti, which stands near the plaza at what is now 516 Polk Street.   Built in the late 1830s by José Amesti, a prominent citizen of the town and owner of a large ranch in the Salinas Valley, the big, two-story adobe, with its graceful proportions, well-placed doors and windows and upstairs gallery, is one of the handsomest examples of preconquest domestic architecture that has come down to us.

The story of the house's origin has elements of romance, for Don José had it built and presented it as a wedding present to a favorite daughter upon her marriage to James McKinley, a Yankee cooper who had become a resident of the province.   The house remained in possession of descendants of the couple until 1918, when it was purchased by Frances Elkins, a noted decorator, who was responsible for the furnishing and interior fittings of many of the most important buildings on the Monterey peninsula, both public and private.

Upon acquiring the property, Mrs. Elkins set about a carefully conceived program of restoration.   As a result, the structure is now one of the historic attractions of the town, its strong walls and spacious chambers having an authenticity that makes it easy for present-day visitors to visualize the manner of life lived there a century or more ago.   The planting of the exterior is especially striking, the line of plane trees before its brick sidewalk and the adjacent row of tall cypresses forming a marked contrast to the white walls of its façade.

It is, however, the garden in the rear that historic-minded visitors find particularly interesting.   For there, as in virtually all California residences of the Spanish and Mexican periods, the family of the first residents and their guests spent a great deal of time, regularly congregating there in the coolness of the long summer evenings.   There meals were eaten; there the children played and the women busied themselves with their embroideries and other prim household tasks. There, too, on occasion, the guitars, *bandurras*, or other stringed instruments were brought forth and there followed a period of singing, or perhaps an impromptu fandango, that lasted far into the night.

9. Casa Amesti, Monterey. One of the handsomest and best preserved of Monterey's adobes is the Amesti house, which stands on Polk Street, a block from the old Plaza. Built in the late 1830s by José Amesti as a wedding gift to his daughter, it remained in possession of the family for many years before passing to a new owner, Mrs. Frances Elkins, under whose direction it was skillfully rehabilitated, both inside and out.
Photograph by Lee Blaisdell, Monterey

The garden of the Amesti-Elkins adobe forms an appropriate setting for such festivities. Sheltered by high, tile-capped walls from the winds blowing in from the bay, its paths and flower beds and venerable, wide-spreading fig trees and clipped hedges make it in truth a private domain, seemingly far removed from the cares and stresses of the world outside.

A few miles off Coast Highway 101, about midway between San Luis Obispo and Santa Barbara, is to be seen one of the most picturesque of California ranch houses dating from before the American Conquest. Located at Los Alamos, the 50,000-acre estate granted José de la Guerra by Mexican Governor Alvarado in 1839, the old casa retains to this day much the appearance it presented when it was built well over a century ago. Thus it stands as a sort of symbol of how the first families of the province lived during the period when California was still a remote Mexican outpost, virtually unknown to the world at large.

Don José, who had recently married Doña Concepción Ortega, one of the belles of Santa Barbara, had the big ranch house built on his newly acquired estate, employing for that purpose the natives of an Indian village located on the property. There he lived for the rest of his life and, upon his death, the house and much of the lands of the original grant passed to his brother-in-law, Gaspar Orena. During the years prior to the annexation of the territory to the United States, great herds of cattle ranged over the hills and valleys of Los Alamos, and each season many loads of hides and tallow were transported in the crude, ox-drawn carts of the period to the beach at San Luis Obispo. There they were transferred to the holds of Yankee trading ships anchored offshore, their owner taking in exchange goods brought out from Boston and other New England ports: furniture for the casa, fabrics and jewelry for the ladies of the household, clothing, firearms, and ammunition for the men, and much else.

PART I: SPANISH AND MEXICAN ADOBES

It was an éra of lavish hospitality on the part of the landowners of the province, and Los Alamos Ranch was long a favorite overnight stopping place for wayfarers passing over El Camino Real between the settlements to the north and south. Not only were these travelers assured of a gracious welcome, but still-existing accounts by some of these early guests make it clear that the hacienda possessed comforts, and even elegancies, rarely encountered in the then remote frontier. For in the big, high-ceilinged rooms were to be seen not only furniture carried out aboard the Boston ships, but antique chests, tables, paintings, and other family heirlooms brought from Spain to Mexico many years earlier and transported over hundreds of miles of mountain and desert trails to California.

The historic adobe passed in due course to a daughter of Don Gaspar Orena, Serena Orena de Koch, who patiently restored it, installing the conveniences required for modern living without doing violence to the appearance it presented during the days when it had been occupied by its original owners. Today the old structure presents, inside and out, an admirable picture of the gracious manner of life lived on certain of the California ranchos during the late eighteenth and early nineteenth centuries.

Of the many relics of Spanish-Mexican days still to be seen in Santa Barbara, one of the most interesting is the de la Guerra residence, a long, one-story adobe structure which faces De la Guerra Street a few yards to the east of State Street in the midst of the present retail shopping district. Today the building, carefully restored and redolent of the days of the town's beginnings, is occupied by the shops and studios of antique dealers and other merchants carrying goods appropriate to this historic setting.

The casa, dating from the early 1820s, was long the home of its original builder and owner, José Antonio Julian de la Guerra y Norigga, a leading citizen of the town and owner of four large ranches in the

10. Casa Carrillo, Santa Barbara. One of Santa Barbara's many historic shrines, this picturesque little adobe dates from the latter 1820s. Here was born Isobel Larkin, said to have been the first child of American parents to be born in California.
Photograph from the Title Insurance & Trust Co., Los Angeles

11. Covarrubias Adobe, Santa Barbara. One of the best preserved of Santa Barbara's many relics of Spanish and Mexican days is this little residence, located at 715 Santa Barbara Street between De la Guerra and Ortega. The date of its building is uncertain, some authorities placing it as early as 1817 and others in the mid-1830s. *Photograph by Karl Obert, Santa Barbara*

area, having a combined total of some 216,000 acres. Born in Spain, de la Guerra arrived in California from Mexico in 1806, a lieutenant with the Spanish forces charged with the occupation and protection of the province. In 1815 he was appointed commandante of the Santa Barbara presidio, a post he continued to hold for nearly three decades. A man of warm and friendly disposition, he well exemplified the gracious hospitality of the Californians of that period, and many early-day visitors to Santa Barbara have left behind a record of pleasant hours spent under his roof. Among the latter was Richard Henry Dana, who during his stay on the coast in the mid-1830s was present at the wedding of a de la Guerra daughter and who, in *Two Years Before the Mast*, gives an account of the colorful reception and ball that followed the ceremony.

In recent years there has sprung up about the old casa a group of white-plastered, tile-roofed buildings that skillfully harmonize with its architectural style, the whole forming a spot where residents and visitors alike delight to shop and dine and take their ease in a setting reminiscent of Old Spain.

Two other interesting examples of Spanish colonial architecture in Santa Barbara, both in an excellent state of preservation, are the Carrillo Adobe at 15 East Carrillo Street, half a block east of State Street, and the Covarrubias House at 715 Santa Barbara Street, between De la Guerra and Ortega.

The first-named was built in the late 1830s by Daniel Hill. Hill was a New Englander who had settled in the province some years earlier and married a daughter of the Ortegas, one of the prominent families of the town. During the next quarter-century the house passed through several hands, eventually coming into the possession of the Carrillos and, after the American Conquest, serving for a time as the meeting place of Santa Barbara's first town council.

The Covarrubias House, dating from the mid-1830s, has frequently been pointed out as one of the finest existing examples of California domestic architecture of the period before the taking over of the province by the Yankees. Built by one of the first citizens of the little community, it was throughout its early years a center of conviviality, the scene of innumerable parties, balls, and other festivities of the fun-loving populace.

The fact that it, unlike so many other of the state's early adobes, has so well withstood the passage of the years, is due to an unusual feature of its construction; namely, that no windows pierced its thick earthen walls, light being admitted to the interior by means of skylights set into the roof. The result was that sunshine, abundant in that area at all seasons of the year, kept the inner sides of the walls dry and in large measure prevented the deterioration that would otherwise have taken place.

Another novel feature of the house is that when, after many years of neglect, it was recently restored, the usual outer coating of plaster was omitted. Thus visitors can see the method of construction employed by California builders of Spanish and Mexican days, for the house's outer walls, reinforced at intervals by massive buttresses, are composed of adobe bricks laid in horizontal rows and joined together by a mortar made of lime mixed with seashells.

Upon its reconstruction, much of the interior was thrown into a single room, a spacious chamber, the dominant feature of which is a huge fireplace at one end. Its white walls, dark tiled floor, and the sturdy, hand-hewn rafters of its roof form a singularly appropriate setting for the antique Spanish tables, chairs and pictures with which the present owner has furnished it.

Santa Barbara has a number of other outstanding relics of the Days of the Dons. The most impressive is, of course, the mission itself, a massive structure surmounted by two belfry towers, which stands facing Los Olivos Street between Garden and Laguna. This is the third church to occupy the site. The first was a temporary chapel put up in 1787 and the second an abode building with tile roof, which replaced

12. Interior, Covarrubias Adobe. Handsomely restored and furnished with pieces appropriate to the period, this room may be considered typical of the living quarters of the town's first citizens a century and more ago. That the little building so well withstood the passage of the years is said to have been due to the fact that it had skylights in its roof, which served to keep the interior dry. *Photograph by Karl Obert, Santa Barbara*

it some seven years later. The latter was partially wrecked by a severe earthquake in 1812. Thereupon, the mission community having meanwhile become one of the largest and most active in the province, with 1700 Indian neophytes living there and attending its shops and gardens and herds, work was at once begun on the present big structure, which was completed and dedicated in 1820.

On East Canon Perdito Street stands El Cuartel, once one of the group of buildings on the grounds of the early presidio. It was built in the early 1780s and is generally regarded as the oldest of the adobes still standing in Santa Barbara. Despite the fact that its appearance has been much changed by later alterations, the little structure, with its thick walls and red-tiled roof, its simple lines and deeply recessed doors and windows, retains more than a suggestion of how it looked when it was originally built more than 170 years ago.

Tradition has it that El Cuartel was erected on the orders of Captain José Francisco de Ortega, first commandante of the newly created Santa Barbara presidio. One of a row of similar structures housing the garrison stationed there, it stood at the end closest to the presidio gate and served as headquarters of the guard, whose duty it was to check on the soldiers and others passing in or out of the compound. Following the taking over of the province by Mexico in 1822, military discipline — never very strict even under Spanish rule — was still further relaxed, and the Santa Barbara post gradually fell into disuse, the former gatehouse becoming the residence of a family named Valenzuela.

The old structure has been continuously occupied ever since, its two rooms, the largest some 15 by 25 feet, serving first as the dwelling place of a succession of owners and in recent years, as the headquarters of the Boy Scout troops in the Santa Barbara area. During the days when it was occupied by the Valenzuela family, a well stood in the patio before the smaller of the two rooms; from it those living in the neighborhood obtained their water. Recently the old patio has been restored, planted to trees and shrubs, with a pool in its center. To assure privacy for this attractive retreat, a high wall was erected, shutting it off from the street.

Facing Laguna Street, a short distance to the north of the present business district, stands yet another of Santa Barbara's group of century-old adobes which add a quaint, old-world look to this picturesque sea-side town. Built in the 1820s by Rafael Gonzales, owner of much land in the area and at one time alcalde — or mayor — of the settlement, upon his death it was inherited by his daughter, who had married a man named Ramirez, and who continued to live there for many years. Not until shortly before her death in the early 1920s did the property pass into other hands.

In its general outlines the old building follows closely the style of the more pretentious residences of the period, being built in the form of a rectangle with L's extending out at either end, and with the doors of the various rooms opening onto covered arcades in front and rear. The casa itself is of generous size; its earthen walls — which vary from two to four feet in thickness — enclose an area approximately 90 by 35 feet and contain seven spacious rooms. The largest, central room has doorways giving access to the garden facing the street on one side and into the semi-enclosed patio in the rear.

When, in the early 1920s, the property was acquired by a new owner, an extensive program of rehabilitation got under way. This, unlike certain other latter-day reconstructions of Spanish or Mexican casas, was carried out with much skill, and every care was taken that in the process of modernization nothing be done to alter its original outlines. The consequence is that, while possessing all the comforts and conveniences of modern living, the old building retains, inside and out, much of the languorous charm of California life during colonial days.

Another well-preserved early California ranch house, and one long revered for its literary associations, is the venerable Camulos hacienda that stands amid an orange grove in the Santa Clara River Valley some thirty miles east of the town of Ventura. The history of the place goes back to the year 1839 when a great area of land, comprising some

13. Camulos Adobe, Ventura County. This charming ranch house, lying some thirty miles to the east of Ventura, is one of the best known in the southern part of the state, for here was laid much of the action of Helen Hunt Jackson's famous novel *Ramona.* Built in the early 1860s by Antonio del Valle,the old house has ever since been admirably maintained inside and out and today presents much the same appearance it did when it was first constructed nearly a century ago. *Photograph from the Title Insurance & Trust Co., Los Angeles*

48,000 acres, and known as the San Francisco Rancho, was granted by the governor of the province, Juan Bautista Alvarado, to Antonio del Valle, an officer in the Mexican army.

Of their original large holdings the del Valles long retained some 2,000 acres, and on these Don Antonio's son Ygnacio put up in the early 1860s the charming adobe that still stands. Throughout the early years guests there were numerous, due both to the traditional hospitality of the Spanish-Mexican rancheros and to the fact that the Camulos adobe stood midway between two pioneer mission settlements, that of San Buenaventura on the coast and San Fernando in the valley of that name, some thirty miles farther inland. Travelers passing that way rarely failed to break their journey by an overnight stop at the rancho.

One visitor to the spot was Helen Hunt Jackson, who stopped there briefly in 1881 and who was so much impressed by what she saw that in her novel *Ramona*, published three years later, she laid much of the action of the story there and, it is said, modeled several of its characters after members of the del Valle family.

Like most of the more pretentious ranch houses of that period and earlier, the Camulos adobe is built about a patio laid out in flower beds and graveled walks, and it was there, and on the verandas facing this central court, that the family and their guests foregathered on the mild evenings that are frequent in that locality the year around. There, too, in the first years was concentrated much of the life of the rancho. "All the kitchen work, except the actual cooking, was done here, in front of the kitchen doors and windows," wrote Helen Hunt Jackson. "Babies slept, were washed, sat in the dirt, and played on the veranda. The women said their prayers, took their naps, and wove their lace there. . . . The herdsmen and shepherds smoked there, lounged there, trained their dogs there."

The tremendous popularity *Ramona* presently came to enjoy made the old adobe a literary shrine and for many years visitors to the spot were welcomed by members of the del Valle family, who continued to

live there until the mid-1920s. Since passing into other hands, however, the house is no longer open to the public. In 1955 a marker, com-
memorating the historical and literary importance of the spot was
erected there by the Native Sons and Daughters of the Golden West.

Continuing on to the south, one presently comes to yet another
early ranch house that has recently been restored and once more serves
its original purpose as a private residence. This historic casa stands
in the San Fernando Valley to the north of Los Angeles and but a short
distance from the San Fernando Mission. Originally built at an un-
determined date in the early 1800s, the old structure presently came
into the possession of General Andrés Pico, son of Pio Pico, one of the
last Mexican governors of the province. In 1873 Andrés Pico and his
adopted son, Don Romulo, undertook extensive alterations on the building, adding the second story and the two wings that enclose the patio
in the rear. Later, the property having passed to other owners, the
old house long stood untenanted and gradually fell into ruin.

When, in the early 1930s, the venerable adobe was acquired by
M. R. Harrington, noted archeologist and curator of the Southwest
Museum in Los Angeles, little remained save its sturdy walls, for its roof,
portico and inner partitions had disappeared and its once well-tended
patio garden was a jungle of weeds. In carrying out his program of
restoration, Dr. Harrington was careful to use only the materials and
methods employed by the Spanish and Mexican artisans of an earlier
day. Because the rains of more than half a century had washed away
hundreds of adobe bricks atop the walls, the new owner set about
searching for someone who could restore the walls to their original
condition. He found the man he was looking for in the person of an
ancient Mexican who, using the soil of the yard re-enforced with straw,
fashioned thousands of bricks which he patiently dried in the sun, and
laid in successive layers to bring the walls back to their former height.

Other phases of the reconstruction were carried out in the same
manner. Roof rafters and the timbers supporting the second floor were

14. Andrés Pico Adobe, San Fernando. One of the most
recent of the traditional Spanish adobes is the one shown above,
erected by Andrés Pico in 1873 on a part of the extensive lands
once owned by him in that area. In 1929, the house, fast
falling to ruin, was purchased by M. R. Harrington, curator
of the Southwest Museum, who skillfully restored it to its
original condition.   *Photograph by Dave Packwood, Los Angeles*

far larger than are customarily used in modern times, the floor joists being 4 by 8 inches. The roof itself was made of hand-split redwood shakes, as research had disclosed that tiles, while almost invariably used on the mission buildings, were rarely employed on the roofs of the ranch houses.

Because of the punctilious manner in which they were carried out, these rebuilding operations required many months, but upon their completion the old casa was widely recognized as an authentic reproduction of an early California ranch house, and remains so the present day.

The group of missions founded by the Spanish friars in the late eighteenth and early nineteenth centuries had for their primary purpose the Christianization of the California Indians. But for all their piety, the missionaries were also men of broad vision, well aware of the practicalities of life on the remote frontier. Hence from the beginning they recognized that religious instruction was but a part of their responsibility. To make their charges useful members of the little communities, it was necessary also to teach them the ways of civilization. Thus at each of the missions there sprang up a cluster of smaller buildings in which the neophytes learned a variety of simple trades: sewing, cooking, the making of adobe bricks, carpentry, weaving, the tanning of leather, and the like. Others were taught to set out and attend the mission gardens, orchards, and vineyards, to plant the surrounding fields to wheat, barley, and maize and to watch over the herds of cattle on the extensive grazing ranges beyond.

With the passage of time the living quarters of the Indians and the workrooms where they practiced their trades for the most part disappeared, with only the big, massively constructed mission buildings themselves remaining as reminders of the varied activities once carried on there. Here and there, however, there exist relics of that phase of the missions' operations, sturdy structures that have somehow survived the wear and tear of the years and the vandalism of later settlers in the areas.

One of the most picturesque and historically important of these is the old mill, El Molino Viejo, once a part of the extensive operations carried on at the San Gabriel Mission near present-day Pasadena. Built about 1810 by the resourceful Spanish friar, José Maria de Zalvidea, it is said to have been the first water-power gristmill ever put up in California. Standing in a shallow depression at the juncture of two arroyos now known as Los Robles and Mill Cañon, it is a sturdy, two-story building, its walls of stone and adobe bricks five feet thick at their base, and its roof of red tiles supported by heavy, hand-hewn timbers.

On the lower floor were the great wooden wheels over which the water, stored in a cistern above, passed, and, as they revolved, turned the heavy millstones in the chamber above. In the mill, which measures approximately 20 by 50 feet, were ground the grain and corn raised in the mission fields, superseding the laborious hand operations formerly in use. The mill had, however, one defect; namely, that the water from the wheels splashed upward and so dampened the newly ground meal that it had to be removed and dried before being stored away for future use. The result was that in 1823 a new mill was constructed nearby and the old one abandoned.

With the secularization of the missions in 1834 and the gradual scattering of the padres and their Indian charges, the old mill fell into disrepair. Finally, a dozen years later, in 1846, the land on which it stood was sold by the Mexican authorities to two residents of the province, William Workman and Hugo Reid, the first a Missourian and the second a native of Scotland. Thereafter the property passed through several hands, eventually coming into the possession of a fire-eating Southerner named Edward J. C. Kewen, who a few years earlier had taken part in William Walker's filibustering campaigns in Nicaragua and Honduras.

15.   El Molino Viejo, San Gabriel.   This historic structure, standing near the site of the present Huntington Hotel, is said to have been the first water-operated gristmill in California. Built about 1810, its walls of sturdy masonry, it was reconstructed in the early 1900s and now serves as a private residence. *Photograph from the Title Insurance & Trust Co., Los Angeles*

Kewen at once set about transforming the old mill into a residence, enlarging the windows on its ground floor, installing French doors and a fireplace in the converted living room, and setting out trees and shrubs on its grounds. He and his wife lived there off and on until his death in 1879, when it was again sold. Eventually, in 1903, it came into the possession of Henry E. Huntington, nephew of the railroad builder, Collis P. Huntington. Henry Huntington was a very large landowner throughout the region and the donor of the great Huntington Library and Art Gallery at San Marino.

Later the old mill again fell on evil days, its successive owners either allowing it to stand vacant or using it as a storehouse or as a place to house crews of laborers. Then, in 1927, the property came into the hands of its present owners, Mr. and Mrs. James R. Brehm, who engaged an architect noted for his skillful work in restoring other adobes of the region, with instructions to convert it into a residence and at the same time preserve as nearly as possible the appearance and feeling of the original structure.

How successfully that difficult assignment was carried out is at once apparent to those who visit the spot today. For despite extensive alterations to meet the requirements of modern living, the building, now close to a century and a half old, retains the flavor of the long-vanished age when it was first put up. For in its reconstruction both the materials and methods used by the early artisans were faithfully followed, with the interior rooms finished in the colors and designs employed by the Indian craftsmen of Mission days and the walled-in garden replanted with the trees and shrubs and flowers known to the padres and their Indian pupils.

Of El Molino Viejo, now registered by the state of California as one of the state's historic sites, the eminent historian, Robert Glass Cleland, has written thus: "Today, in a world of confusion, uncertainty, and fear, [its walls] stand as a symbol of things not temporal but eternal — a pledge and promise of the ancient but half-forgotten truth that if a man build with integrity and faith his handiwork will somehow survive the ruin of the years."

Another historic adobe in the Los Angeles area, this one within the borders of the present city of Long Beach, is Los Alamitos ("The Little Cottonwoods"), which stands close to the San Gabriel River. Originally it was part of an immense land grant that, in 1784, was awarded to Manuel Nieto, a former soldier who had served under Governor Fages. Nieto ran great herds of horses and cattle over his property; then, upon his death in 1804, it was divided into two parts, the northern half called Los Cerritos, going to his daughter Manuela, and Los Alamitos to his son, Juan José.

Don José held title to Los Alamitos for some three decades, then sold it to the governor of the province, José Figueroa, the consideration being $500 in gold. Figueroa's plan of living there was, however, not realized, for he died at Monterey the following year, and in 1842 the rancho again changed hands. The purchase price this time was hides and tallow to the value of $5,500, the buyer being Abel Sterns, one of a group of young New Englanders who had come out to California in the late 1820s and early 1830s, married the daughters of local families —in his case the beauteous Doña Arcadia Bandini—and had taken out Mexican citizenship.

The Sternses remained in possession of the rancho, which comprised some 29,000 acres, for more than two decades, raising horses, sheep, and cattle there and frequently exchanging visits with their neighbors, the Temples, who lived nearby at Los Cerritos. In the early 1860s, however, a series of abnormally dry winters brought disaster, the death of thousands of head of livestock bringing ruin to their once prosperous owners. When, in 1865, the big Los Alamitos Rancho was advertised for sale to pay delinquent taxes—only $153—there were no takers, and the title passed to Michael Reese, holder of a mortgage on the property.

Reese, who lived in San Francisco, proceeded to rent Los Alamitos,

16. Courtyard of the Pio Pico House, near Whittier. Beside Highway 101 a short distance from the town of Whittier stands this interesting adobe, the home of Pio Pico, last of California's Mexican governors and at one time reputed to be the wealthiest man in the province. The house, now a state monument, has recently been completely restored. *Photograph from the Title Insurance & Trust Co., Los Angeles*

and thus in 1878 a part of it was leased to John W. Bixby, a relative of the Bixbys who had become part owners of the adjoining Los Cerritos Rancho. Thereupon John Bixby, with his wife and young son Fred, moved into the little adobe ranch house which, having been unoccupied for more than a decade, was in a deplorable state. Years later, Sarah Bixby Smith, niece of John Bixby, recalled that the pretty gardens set out by Mrs. Sterns had fallen to ruin, that the largest room of the casa had been used as a calf-pen, and that the entire premises were overrun by hordes of rats.

At once, however, the young couple set about renovating the little structure, enlarging the windows and cutting doors in its thick adobe walls, restoring the garden, and installing a bathroom. Later, having meantime acquired the property from the Reese heirs, further improvements were made: the building of a wing containing two bedrooms, the moving of the dining room and kitchen to a second addition, the planting of a cactus garden, the installation of heating and water systems. When, in due course the property passed to the son, Fred Bixby, this program of improvement was carried forward, with the result that today Los Alamitos is widely recognized to be one of the most charming, and authentic, restorations of early California ranch houses to be found anywhere in the state.

Some eighteen miles to the northeast of Long Beach, and a short distance from the town of Whittier, is the venerable adobe that was once the home of Pio Pico, the last Mexican governor of the province. Pico, born at nearby San Gabriel in 1801, fled to Mexico when the Americans conquered the territory. He returned to California, however, two years later and presently built, on property called El Ranchito, the comfortable residence that still stands. Laid out in the form of a U, with the lower floor of adobe bricks and the second story of wood, it has long been one of the historic houses of the area. Its owner and builder lived to a venerable age, dying in 1894. Today the old house, the view of which is obscured from the highway by a line of trees, has a marker setting forth the prominent part Pio Pico played in the early history of the state.

Within the present city of Los Angeles, near the corner of Third and Fairfax streets, is another interesting adobe, which, admirably restored, still serves as a private dwelling. Erected in 1828 by Antonio José Rocha, a blacksmith by trade, who had reached the province from his native Portugal in 1815, the house stood on what had once been a part of the Los Angeles pueblo lands. Later, a portion of these lands was granted to Rocha and became known as the Rancho La Brea because of the fact that on the property were a number of spots where considerable quantities of brea — that is, crude oil — rose to the surface. It is interesting to recall that throughout that early period all transfers of title to the property contained the stipulation that residents of the Los Angeles pueblo were to be allowed to take from the brea pits enough of that substance to make waterproof the roofs of their casas.

In the fall of 1860 the old Rocha adobe, together with the lands that surrounded it, was deeded to a family named Hancock, and with the rise of the oil industry a few years later vast quantities of petroleum were extracted from the property. Eventually, however, the oil fields were exhausted, and today the region is occupied by the broad, tree-lined streets and attractive homes of the Wilshire district. The thick-walled, tile-roofed adobe, now more than a century and a quarter old, is one of the most charming residences of the area. It has been skillfully rehabilitated by the oil magnate, Earl C. Gilmore, who was born within its venerable walls.

Another of the many old adobes still to be seen in the Los Angeles area is the little Sanchez casa, located in the town of Glendale some half-mile to the west of the north end of Brand Boulevard. The land on which it stands was once a portion of the Rancho San Rafael, the first Spanish grant to be made in California, assigned in 1784 to José

17. La Brea Ranch House, Los Angeles. Built more than 125 years ago, this old adobe, skillfully restored, stands in the midst of one of Los Angeles's most attractive residential districts and still serves its original purpose as a private dwelling.

Photograph from the Title Insurance & Trust Co., Los Angeles

18. Sanchez Adobe, Glendale. Occupying land that was once part of the huge Rancho San Rafael, this little structure was long the home of Thomas A. Sanchez, sheriff of Los Angeles County during pioneer days. *Photograph from the Title Insurance & Trust Co., Los Angeles*

19. Garcia Adobe, Capistrano. On the present Highway 101, about midway between Los Angeles and San Diego and adjacent to the San Juan Capistrano Mission, stands this excellent example of California domestic architecture of pre-Conquest days. Built in the 1840s by Don Manuel Garcia, it was acquired in the 1880s by Domingo Oyharzabal, wealthy Basque sheepman, who restored it to its original condition.
Photograph from the Title Insurance & Trust Co., Los Angeles

Maria Verdugo and having an area of 36,000 acres. Today half a dozen towns, including Glendale, Eagle Rock, and Verdugo City, occupy its site.

Later the great estate was divided among the heirs of its original owner and thus a 50-acre piece presently came into the possession of the former Maria Sepulveda, then the wife of Thomas A. Sanchez, noted early-day sheriff of Los Angeles County, The little adobe they built there in the mid-1870s still survives, a grove of tall eucalyptus trees in its front yard and its windows commanding a view of the rugged Verdugo hills in the background.

Close to the seacoast and about midway between Los Angeles and San Diego stands the picturesque village of San Juan Capistrano, grouped about the ruins of the old mission of that name — the latter one of the most impressive and extensive of the series of churches and attendant buildings put up by the Franciscan fathers in the late eighteenth and early nineteenth centuries. Of the score or more still existing adobe residences erected by the early Spanish or Mexican settlers in the vicinity, one of the largest and best preserved is that known as the Garcia-Oyharzabal House. Adjacent to Highway 101, the much-traveled thoroughfare that parallels the coast from one end of the state to the other, the big, two-story structure was built in the 1840s by one Don Garcia, long a resident of the area. Sometime in the 1880s it was purchased by a wealthy Basque sheepman named Domingo Oyharzabal and the historic dwelling, carefully restored and kept in excellent condition, has ever since remained in possession of the family.

When, in the summer of 1769, Father Junipero Serra founded the first mission on California soil, he prepared the way for the first town to be established within the borders of that then remote Spanish province. For soon thereafter the soldiers who had accompanied the expedition from Mexico laid out a military post, or presidio, on a little hill overlooking San Diego Bay. Their purpose was both to protect the mission from attack by Indians and to ward off possible attempts by foreign powers to lay claim to the country.

In due course the civilian population of the small settlement began building their adobe residences on a site at the foot of Presidio Hill, grouping them in the manner of their homeland, about the four sides of a central plaza. In this area, known to present-day San Diegans as "Old Town," are still to be seen a number of picturesque structures dating from before the American Conquest.

One of the most interesting and historically important of these is the Casa Estudillo, built in 1826 by José Antonio Estudillo, the scene of frequent entertainments by its hospitable, pleasure-loving owners. The old house was well adapted to the accommodation of guests, for not only did it contain twelve spacious rooms but these were ranged about a central courtyard in which many of the festive events were held. In addition, throughout that earlier period, the one-story structure boasted an elevated tower, or cupola, which commanded a view of the town's plaza opposite; there on gala occasions the guests would assemble to witness the bullfights and other events held in the square.

The old adobe has long been celebrated not only for the beauty of its proportions and the quaint charm of its old-world patio, but for its literary and historical associations. Helen Hunt Jackson made it the scene of much of the action of her novel of California Indian life, with the result that the casa is often referred to as "Ramona's Marriage Place." Its historic importance lies mainly in the fact that when the United States forces took possession of San Diego in 1846, the women and children of the pueblo sought refuge there during the brief exchange of gunfire that preceded the town's fall.

In 1910 the old house, which years of neglect had reduced to a partial ruin, was acquired by T. P. Getz. Its new owner not only carefully restored it to its original condition but assembled in the rooms and patio a notable collection of furniture, paintings, Indian relics,

20. Casa de Estudillo, San Diego. This venerable adobe, built in the mid-1820s, well illustrates the plan on which the more pretentious homes of the period were laid out, its twelve rooms being grouped about three sides of a patio.   *Photograph from the Union Title Insurance & Trust Co., San Diego*

household utensils, and similar articles dating from Spanish and Mexican days. Today the venerable structure is maintained as a public museum, one that affords visitors an opportunity to visualize the manner of life lived there in the days when California was an isolated Mexican province.

Adjacent to the Estudillo house stands one of the largest, and historically most important, adobes fronting on the plaza of San Diego's Old Town. This is the Casa de Bandini, which with its spacious rooms and broad balconies is an excellent example of its type. Built in the mid-1820s by Juan Bandini, a native of Peru, who had long been a figure of prominence in the territory, it was originally but one story high; not until the late 1860s was the second floor added.

By all accounts, the Bandini casa was a center of gaiety during the two decades prior to the American Conquest, for its owner was a man of markedly convivial instincts and he had besides a brood of pretty, fun-loving daughters. Fandangos, *tertulias*, and other festive gatherings were frequent and there is ample evidence that they were well attended. The historian, Hubert H. Bancroft, quotes Don Juan's wife as having once stated that so numerous were their guests that there were occasions when at mealtime their table, which seated forty, had to be set twice.

The house figured prominently, too, in events leading up to the taking over of California by the Americans. It was there that Commodore Robert F. Stockton, in command of the naval forces in the Pacific, set up his headquarters, and there, on December 9, 1846, Lieutenant Beale and the famous scout, Kit Carson, arrived bringing news of the desperate plight of General Kearny's troops following the battle of San Pascual, some thirty-five miles to the north. Re-enforcements were promptly dispatched to the hard-pressed Kearny forces and three days later the bedraggled caravan, many of its members wounded and all footsore and hungry, reached San Diego.

51

21. Casa de Pedrorena, San Diego. Said to have been the first frame house in San Diego, this was built in the late 1830s for Miguel de Pedrorena, a man of excellent family and education, who arrived in the province in 1838 and married one of the belles of the town, Maria Antonia Estudillo. *Photograph from the Union Title Insurance & Trust Co., San Diego*

PART I: SPANISH AND MEXICAN ADOBES

The Bandinis were one of the native families that favored the taking over of California by the United States — it having grown clear that Mexico's hold on the province could not be much longer maintained — and it is recorded that the daughters of the household made the American flag that was raised above the plaza of the Old Town earlier that year.

Throughout the 1860s the house was the terminus of a number of stage lines and, following the building of the second story in 1869, it became the Cosmopolitan Hotel, long a leading hostelry of the town. In recent years it has come into the possession of a grandson of its original owner, who carefully restored it. It is still operated as a hotel.

Yet another of the historic residences standing in San Diego's Old Town is the Casa de Pedrorena, a picturesque small house that is said to have been the first frame building to be put up there. Its original owner was Miguel de Pedrorena, a man of education and gracious manners, who, born in Madrid, had reached the little frontier community in 1838. Soon after his arrival he formed a romantic attachment for Maria Antonio, one of the daughters of José Antonio Estudillo whose large adobe fronted on the plaza nearby, and it was to this cottage that he took his bride. Today the Pedrorena casa, well over a century old, is still occupied and kept in excellent repair, its large grounds, enclosed in an adobe wall, handsomely laid out and forming a favorite gathering place for the residents during the long San Diego summers.

Built at a somewhat later date than the Pedrorena casa, but similar to it in size and design, is another cottage called the Pendleton house, which faces one of the streets of the Old Town. Tradition has it that it was erected in 1852 by Juan Bandini and presented to his daughter Dolores upon her marriage to a Captain Charles Johnson. The house is best known, however, as the residence of George Horatio Derby, an army engineer and early-day humorist, who wrote under the name of John Phoenix, and whose *Phoenixiana* went through many editions and is still read and admired today.

Some of Derby's stunts have become classics of Western humor, as when in 1853 the owner of the first San Diego newspaper, the *Herald*, departed on a trip to San Francisco, leaving Derby in charge. During the other's absence Derby filled the journal's news columns with humorous anecdotes, reversed its stand on political questions, and in its editorials advocated all manner of preposterous measures. Evidently he was forgiven that transgression, however, for he continued to contribute to the paper after its owner's return.

Derby occupied the little cottage from 1853 to 1855. In the mid-1860s it was sold to another prominent resident of the Old Town, Captain George Allen Pendleton, who had married one of the Estudillo daughters, Concepción, and who lived there until his death in 1871. During much of that period Pendleton held the posts of county clerk and county recorder and the house served both as his residence and office.

22.   Pendleton House, San Diego.   This little cottage in San Diego's Old Town was built in 1852 by Juan Bandini and presented to his daughter Dolores upon her marriage.   It is chiefly remembered, however, as the residence of the early-day humorist, George Derby, and later of Captain George Pendleton.
Photograph from the Union Title Insurance & Trust Co., San Diego

PART

II

THE COMING OF THE FOREIGNERS

By no means all the California residences dating from the period before the Yankees took over in 1846 were put up by natives of Spain or Mexico. For beginning a full third of a century before the American Conquest, a group of far-ranging adventurers from other countries, chiefly the United States, England, and France, had settled there, most of them marrying Mexican wives, taking out Mexican citizenship, and, when it came time to build permanent homes, choosing the style of architecture most widely used in their adopted country.

For by and large the newcomers found the adobe casas, with their thick walls, covered verandas, and semi-enclosed patios, singularly well adapted to the California climate, particularly in the central and southern parts of the province, and their own dwellings accordingly followed the same general plan. To be sure, there were a few who rejected what was to them an alien environment, and from the early 1840s onward there began to appear in the sleepy Mexican pueblos an occasional residence patterned after the houses the owner had known on the streets of his native town. These, however, were the exception rather than the rule and until the transfer of the province to American ownership the adobe brick continued to be by all odds the most widely used building material.

On a windy headland in what is now Sonoma County, a few miles to the north of the mouth of the Russian River, stand the forlorn relics of a colony established there by Imperial Russia close to a century and a half ago. The reason for the founding of this outpost on the wild and remote section of the California coast lay in the fact that Russian fur hunters were then active in the waters off the Aleutian Islands, and it was the purpose to raise in California cattle, wheat, and other food-stuffs needed in their far northern settlements.

Accordingly, in the spring of 1812, a party under the command of Ivan Alexander Kuskof landed at the spot and began the building of a log fort, which was completed in mid-May of that year. Because the Spanish authorities at Monterey looked with suspicion on this attempt by the Russians to establish themselves permanently there, and had even threatened to oust them by force, Kuskof enclosed his little settlement on the bluff with a stockade of heavy timbers, fourteen feet high, at the north and south corners of which were two-story blockhouses in which cannon were mounted.

The anticipated attack, however, never materialized, and for close to three decades the colonists lived there peaceably enough, planting their fields to grain, potatoes, and other crops, and running herds of cattle over the surrounding hills. Within the stockade close to three score buildings were put up, including barracks for the soldiers, a chapel, the commandant's house, shops for blacksmiths and other artisans, warehouses, and a jail. During the early years the settlement prospered moderately, but as time passed, fur-hunting operations farther north went into a decline, less supplies were needed, and in 1841 came orders for its abandonment. Accordingly, the property there was

23. Chapel at Fort Ross, Sonoma County. Only surviving building of the outpost colony established by Russia on the northern California coast in 1812, this little chapel, with its crude belfry and quaint dome, was built from redwood trees growing on the surrounding hillsides. Recently the little building was taken into the state park system and carefully reconstructed according to its original plan. *Photograph by Keith's Studio, Santa Rosa*

24. Sutter's Fort, Sacramento. Handsomely reconstructed
and now a part of the state park system, this group of buildings comprised the headquarters of Captain John A. Sutter,
the first permanent resident of the Sacramento Valley. The
two-story structure to the left was Sutter's home; built in 1839,
it is now a museum containing many relics of pioneer days.
Photograph by McCurry Studios, Sacramento

sold to Johann August Sutter, of Sutter's Fort fame, and the Russians withdrew.

Thereafter for more than half a century the old fort stood vacant, its buildings one by one falling to ruin and the high wall of its stockade slowly rotting away. Then, in the early 1900s, the site was taken over by the state, designated the Fort Ross Historic Monument, and a program of restoration got under way. Today three of the original buildings have been reconstructed: the Greek Orthodox Chapel, one of the old blockhouses, and the commandant's house. The first, a tiny structure of hand-hewn redwood timbers, with belfry and quaint, rounded dome, stands at one corner of the former stockade. Nearby is the commandant's house, also built of roughly hewn timbers, the high-pitched roof of which extends out over the porch in front. The building, with its small rooms and box-like proportions, is quite without distinction architecturally, yet as a reminder of the days when Russia maintained a colony on California soil, it has an interest — and significance — surpassing that of many far more impressive houses.

The purchaser of the Russians' property at Fort Ross was, as stated, Johann August Sutter, whose venerable residence and trading post stands in the midst of a pleasant, wooded park at 26th and L streets in Sacramento.

Sutter, a Swiss emigrant who reached the province in 1839 by way of the Sandwich Islands and Alaska, settled in the Sacramento Valley, then virtually uninhabited save by roving bands of Indians. There he acquired vast tracts of farming and grazing lands and started a large-scale development of his property, which he christened New Helvetia. It was while a group of his employees were building a sawmill in the Sierra foothills that gold was discovered on January 24, 1848, a circumstance that proved disastrous to Sutter, for the horde of miners that presently appeared pre-empted much of his most fertile land, scattered his herds and ended his dream of establishing a permanent empire.

As it stands today, the fort is largely a reconstruction of what it was in the mid-1840s, the only original building being a two-story house of adobe bricks in the center of the enclosure; this, now a museum, once served as the owner's living quarters. Ranged about it, inside the high walls, have been built a group of structures similar to those in which were carried on the varied activities of the fort: a blacksmith shop, granary, and storerooms, together with quarters for employees and visitors, and a room that housed the Indian guardsmen Sutter kept posted before the gates.

The property is now owned and maintained by the state and within its walls have been assembled a wide variety of articles dating from pioneer days. These include letters, land grants, and numerous other documents of the Spanish and Mexican periods; picks, pans, rockers, and like mining tools of the '49ers, together with an assortment of primitive household furniture and utensils once used in the early gold camps.

Of particular interest to present-day visitors is a collection of saddles, spurs, and other relics of the Pony Express riders, that gallant band of hard-riding youths who for a period of nineteen months, beginning in the spring of 1860, carried the mails — at a charge of $5 per ounce — between St. Joseph, Missouri, and Sacramento, traveling day and night and covering the nearly 2,000 miles of barren, Indian-infested territory in eight days or less. Ranged about the buildings inside the walls are many other mementoes of pioneer days: stagecoaches and cumbersome prairie schooners, ornate little hand-operated fire engines used by volunteer companies to combat the frequent fires that swept through the wooden buildings of the early towns and camps, heavy, crudely made millstones from the primitive gristmills of the early 1850s, and much else.

Some 135 miles to the north of Sacramento and a short distance outside the town of Red Bluff stands a quaint little adobe that dates from the 1840s and was long the home of William B. Ide, Yankee

25.   The William B. Ide Adobe, near Red Bluff.   Overlooking
the Sacramento River and sheltered by a grove of ancient oaks,
this little adobe dwelling was built in 1849 by "General"
William B. Ide, who three years earlier had led the party of
American settlers who captured the town of Sonoma and set
up the short-lived Bear Flag Republic.   *Photograph by Harry W.
Abrahams, San Francisco*

26. John Bidwell House, Chico. This residence of General John Bidwell, who arrived in California in 1841 and, after the American conquest, became one of the most influential figures in the new state, stands amid spacious grounds in the town of Chico, which he founded. In recent years it has been used as a girls' dormitory of the Chico State College. *Photograph by Norman Miner, Santa Rosa*

frontiersman who played a leading part in the events that led up to the taking over of the province by the United States toward the middle of that decade.

Ide, a native of Rutland, Massachusetts, came West with one of the pioneer overland parties, settled on lands near the northern end of the Sacramento Valley, and was presently deeply involved in the exploit known to history as the Bear Flag Rebellion. He, indeed, was one of the leaders in that movement, and when, in the spring of 1846, a little band of settlers took possession of the Mexican outpost at Sonoma, he was named president of the California Republic they proceeded to establish. His occupancy of that office was, however, brief. Less than a month later, United States warships sailed into Monterey and San Francisco bays and, on July 9, a detachment of troops reached Sonoma and the American emblem replaced that of the Bear Flaggers.

Following that picturesque interlude, Ide returned to his lands at the northern end of the valley, gradually increased his holdings there, and built the little adobe house that still remains. The house, together with its wooded grounds, has recently been taken into the state park system and preserved, not only for its historic associations, but as an example of the more simple type of ranch house put up by early American settlers in the province.

Later a wooden wing and porch were added to the house, both of which still stand. The original structure, the adobe bricks of its walls visible beneath successive coatings of whitewash, has well withstood the wear and tear of the years and remains to all outward appearances as sturdy as the day it was put up. Throughout the 1850s and 1860s it was a familiar landmark to travelers passing through that region, as it was one of the stopping places on the old stagecoach route between California and Oregon. Moreover, facilities for crossing the Sacramento River at that point were established by Ide in the late 1840s, and the Adobe Ferry — as it came to be called — continued to function until 1876 when an iron bridge was built at nearby Red Bluff.

One feature of the old house rarely fails to engage the interest of visitors. This is a series of rectangular openings extending across its north wall a foot or two below the eaves. Tradition has it that these were designed to enable those within to defend themselves in the event of attack by hostile Indians. There are, however, unromantic souls who offer a more prosaic explanation. They maintain that the so-called loopholes were really niches in which rested the timbers supporting the roof of a porch that once extended across that side of the house. One is, of course, at liberty to accept whichever explanation best suits his temperament.

Long one of the best-known and most widely respected residents of the northern Sacramento Valley was General John Bidwell, member of the first party of immigrants to reach California over the formidable barrier of the Sierra range,and the founder and ever-generous patron of the town of Chico.

Bidwell arrived in the province in 1841, worked for a time for the doughty Swiss adventurer, John Sutter, at what is now Sacramento, then settled on his immense rancho which lay some eighty miles farther up the valley. In later years Bidwell often told the story of how he had come to locate on that remote spot. One night while encamped near where the town of Vacaville now stands, some of the horses belonging to his party were stolen by a group of frontiersmen. Next morning Bidwell set off in pursuit, following their tracks northward up the valley for several days before overtaking them and recovering his property. Impressed by the fertility and beauty of the country traversed, he some years later bought the big Chico rancho and several adjacent properties from their original owners.

There he lived for the remainder of his long life, first in a rude log cabin and, about 1852, in an adobe ranch house, the site of which today is marked by a plaque honoring his memory. Meantime, the town of Chico has sprung up on his property, and he had made his big rancho one of the most productive in the state, running great herds of cattle on the outlying sections, planting fields of wheat and other crops, and setting out extensive orchards and vineyards, being at much pains to select only the best varieties of trees and vines.

Following Bidwell's marriage in 1868, he built the big stone residence, with its broad verandas and lofty tower, that stands today in its grove of stately trees at the edge of the town. During the more than three decades of his marriage, the Bidwell Ranch remained one of the showplaces of northern California, to which were drawn not only those interested in studying the advanced agricultural methods Bidwell had introduced, but many figures prominent in public life, for its owner had made himself a power in political matters as well.

Following his death in 1900, his widow presented the house and its surrounding gardens, together with an extensive area of wooded lands, to the city of Chico, which has ever since maintained it as a public park. In recent years the old homestead, known locally as the "Bidwell Mansion," has served as a dormitory for girl students of the Chico State College.

Beside a highway called Marsh Creek Road, a few miles from the village of Brentwood in Contra Costa County, stands a gaunt, three-story stone structure that figured large in the early history of that region. Built in the middle '50s of the last century, it was intended as the home of John Marsh, owner of the immense Los Medanos Rancho, an area four leagues long and three wide that extended from the banks of the San Joaquin River to the base of Mount Diablo.

Among the little group of United States citizens who took up residence in California during the days when it was ruled by Mexico, Marsh was ever something of an enigma, a puzzle alike to the Mexican officials and ranchers and to his fellow Americans. Born in Massachusetts in the early 1800s, and graduated from Harvard with the class of 1823, he had at once set out for the trans-Mississippi frontier. There

27. John Marsh House, Contra Costa County. This three-story, stone house, standing beside Marsh Creek Road a few miles to the east of Mount Diablo, was built in the early 1850s by Massachusetts-born John Marsh, who had arrived in the province in 1836, set himself up as a frontier doctor (although he had had no medical training) and, exacting cattle in payment of his professional fees, gradually assembled great herds on his property, which he named Rancho los Medanos (The Sandhills). *Photograph from the California Historical Society, San Francisco*

he became in turn Indian agent, schoolteacher, and participant in the Black Hawk War, then pushed on westward and, in 1836, arrived in California. He presented his Harvard degree of Bachelor of Arts to the authorities at the Pueblo of Los Angeles, representing it to be a medical degree. It was accepted as such by the Mexican officials — who could not read its Latin text — and he thereupon set himself up as a physician, the first American M.D. in the province.

Marsh acquired the huge Los Medanos property in 1837 and for the next two decades busied himself both as a cattleman and frontier doctor, visiting the ailing on the widely scattered ranches of the area, and taking as payment cattle to augment his herds at Los Medanos. His usual professional fee was one animal for each mile he had to travel to reach the patient's sickbed.

During the earlier part of his stay at Los Medanos he lived in a modest adobe ranch house, and it was there, in the fall of 1841, that he received the first party of immigrants to reach California via the Overland Trail, a group that numbered one woman, one child, and thirty-two men, among them John Bidwell and several others who later became prominent in California affairs.

Then, in 1851, having prospered mightily and taken a wife, he set about the building of a house more in keeping with his new estate. The site selected was near his old adobe, a spot that commanded a wide view of the plain and mountains and was close to a grove of ancient valley oaks. As materials for his manor house he rejected both the humble adobe bricks of the early Californians and the mill-sawed boards fancied by the newly arrived Yankees. His must be built of imperishable stone, and a crew of Indians was set to work fashioning blocks out of cream-colored sandstone from a nearby quarry.

The house was a long time building, and before it was completed the young bride who was to preside over it sickened and died. As it happened, Marsh himself was destined to occupy it for only a brief period. For in the fall of 1856, while on his way to Martinez to catch a boat for San Francisco, he was set on by a group of robbers and stabbed to death.

Today the house itself stands, forlorn and vacant, by the roadside, a monument alike to human vanity and to the skill and integrity of its builders. For in the hundred years that have passed since its strong walls rose above the surface of the plain, its appearance has changed but little. To be sure, the stonework of the exterior has weathered to a deep brown shade, and here and there the mortar between the blocks has disintegrated and blown away. Moreover, the wooden porch and second-floor gallery that once extended across the front and down one side have long since disappeared, and the sixty-five-foot stone tower that rose above the front door, on the top of which Marsh was wont to stand, field glasses in hand, and keep watch over his grazing herds, was shaken down by an earthquake in 1869 and never rebuilt.

Otherwise the house looks much as it did on the day it was finished. The lowest of its three floors is divided by a wide hall, on the left of which is the living room, forty feet in length, with a fireplace at one end and on two sides tall French doors that once opened onto the porch outside. Across the hall is the dining room, capable, it was said, of comfortably seating forty guests (though there is no record of the frugal owner ever having entertained that many), with the kitchen and service quarters housed in an adjoining wing to the rear. Above is the spacious master bedroom, occupying the same space as the living room downstairs. Adjoining it is an upstairs sitting room designed for the use of the lady of the house, and beyond is a chamber which Marsh planned to fix up as a study and library. The third floor, lighted by windows set into the gables of the roof, was never finished, and was used as an attic storeroom by later tenants of the building.

Of the group of old adobes facing Sonoma's plaza, all put up over a century ago, two are of particular interest, representing as they do the type of residences in which prosperous landowners of the province lived during the years just prior to the American Conquest.

PART II: THE COMING OF THE FOREIGNERS

One of these is the Fitch House, which stands at the southwest corner of the plaza, a two-story adobe of pleasing proportions, having a second-floor balcony across its front with French doors opening into the upstairs bedrooms. The house was built for General Vallejo's brother-in-law, Jacob P. Leese, an Ohio-born merchant who had arrived in the province in the early 1830s and established stores, first at Monterey and then, in 1836, at the outpost village of Yerba Buena on the shore of San Francisco Bay.

When the Bear Flaggers took possession of Sonoma and set up the short-lived California Republic, Leese was one of the town's leading citizens who were rounded up and held prisoners for a few days before being released. Later that same year — 1846 — the house served as headquarters for General Persifor F. Smith, commander of the American forces in the north, and in the 1850s it became a boarding school for girls under the name of St. Mary's Hall. Today the old structure again serves the purpose for which it was originally built; that is, as a private residence.

Also privately owned is the Ray House at the corner of East Spain and Second streets, a commodious, two-story structure, the first section of which, built of wood, was put up in the mid-1840s, and to which a large addition, of adobe bricks, was added a few years later. Like so many of the more pretentious California residences of the period, this one has on the two sides facing the streets a roof projecting some distance beyond its walls and supported by wooden columns, thus converting the sidewalk below into a sort of veranda in the shade of which residents and their guests were wont to congregate.

Something more than a hundred miles to the south of Sonoma, and facing San Juan's old plaza, stands a picturesque building, a big, two-story house with a balcony extending across its façade, that was long the home of Angelo Zanetta, owner of the Plaza Hotel across the way. Although the Zanetta house belongs to a later period than other buildings grouped about the plaza — it was built in the late 1860s —

28. Ray House, Sonoma. Standing at the corner of East
Spain and Second streets is this handsome, well-preserved
residence, the most striking feature of which is the broad, overhanging roof, on its two street frontages, supported by graceful
wooden columns. This roof gives an appearance not unlike
the Southern manor houses of pre-Civil War days. *Photograph by Edgar Waite, Sonoma*

29. Zanetta House, San Juan Bautista. Fronting on San
Juan's plaza is this two-story frame dwelling, with character-
istic second-floor balcony, that was long the home of Angelo
Zanetta, proprietor of the Plaza Hotel across the way.
Photograph by Sigurd Larsen, San Juan Bautista

the spot on which it stands is a historic one, for it was once the site of a commodious adobe put up by the mission fathers in 1815 and known to early residents as the "Nunnery." This name was derived from the fact that it housed the unmarried Indian women of the mission establishment. Here they practised such simple crafts as weaving, sewing, pottery-making and the like.

In 1832 the original building was enlarged and a spacious courtyard, enclosed in a high adobe wall, was built in the rear. Following the secularization of the missions the subsequent year, the structure passed to the control of the civilian authorities of the province and for some time served as a barracks to house a troop of cavalrymen under the command of General José Castro. Then, for several decades after California became a part of the United States, the building remained untenanted and gradually fell into ruin. When Angelo Zanetta acquired the property in 1868 he had what remained of the old adobe torn down and built on the site the sturdy structure that stands today, utilizing many of the bricks from the earlier edifice in the construction of its outer walls.

It is said that when Zanetta built the house plans were afoot to make San Juan the county seat of San Benito County and it was his hope that it would be purchased for use as the county courthouse. When that plan failed to work out, and nearby Hollister became the county seat, the big building was converted to other uses, the upper floor being made into a single large chamber that was long the scene of balls and other social gatherings, and the first story being occupied both by a bar and by living quarters for the owner and his family.

Today the old house, together with the other buildings fronting on the southern and western sides of the plaza, has been acquired by the state and permanently set aside as a historical monument. Under the direction of the State Division of Beaches and Parks, a comprehensive program of restoration has been carried out; the courtyard in the rear has been cleared of later additions and laid out according to its

30. Crane Cottage, San Juan. Not all of San Juan's buildings dating from the early days are grouped about the plaza.
Standing at the corner of Second and Polk streets, and still
in use as a private residence, is this small clapboard cottage,
built in 1857 by a pioneer settler named Crane. *Photograph*
by Sigurd Larsen, San Juan Bautista

original plan, with tables, benches, and other facilities for outdoor living lining the walks beneath the century-old trees. In the downstairs rooms have been assembled furniture, pictures, and household utensils belonging to the period when the house was first built, thus affording visitors an opportunity to visualize the domestic environment in which their forebears lived some eighty-odd years ago.

Singularly rich in historical lore associated with California's early days is the Larkin House, the adobe which stands on the busy Monterey thoroughfare known in Spanish and Mexican days as the Calle Principal and which now bears the prosaic title of Main Street. It was long the home of Thomas O. Larkin, the first — and only — United States Consul in the Mexican province, and generally recognized as one of the ablest, and most influential, American residents of the entire west coast.

One of the little group of shrewd New England traders who had come out to California during the first third of the last century, Larkin reached Monterey in 1832, and was soon conducting a far-ranging and lucrative business there. As head of a thriving mercantile house, to which the mission padres and the owners of the big ranchos of the interior came to exchange their hides and tallow for the goods brought out on the Boston windjammers, Larkin speedily became an important factor in the economic life of the province. But that was not all. For, in addition to his business acumen, he was a man of integrity and broad vision, and these qualities won him the respect and confidence not only of the native ranchers and officials of the province, but of the Americans, British, and other foreigners who were then beginning to make their way into the country.

It was because of his high standing in the community that when, in the mid-1840s, it grew obvious that Mexico's hold on the province could not be much longer maintained, and the authorities at Washington felt the need of a representative at Monterey to keep them informed

31. Larkin House, Monterey. Built in 1835 by Thomas O. Larkin, first — and only — U.S. Consul in the Mexican province, this handsome, two-story adobe served as headquarters of the American forces under Commodore Sloat which took over the town on July 2, 1846. *Photograph by Lee Blaisdell, Monterey*

of the fast-moving events in California, Larkin was the logical choice for that post. He was accordingly appointed United States Consul early in 1844 and served in that capacity during the crowded years that followed. His dispatches to the State Department, together with his amiable relations with the Mexican officials and his prudent counsel to other Americans in the province, played a highly important part in the events leading up to California's transfer to the United States in 1846.

In addition to his other characteristics Larkin was a meticulous keeper of records, and it is because of that quality that we have today the complete history of the building of his Monterey casa, including the cost of every item that went into its construction, down to the last nail. These are set forth in three neatly written account books, covering the period from March 1832 to February 1840, now preserved in the Bancroft Library at the University of California. And a fascinating story they tell, particularly in the light they throw on building costs in California during the Days of the Dons.

From them we learn that Larkin, having decided to build a house in keeping with his position as the town's leading merchant, began collecting construction materials toward the close of 1834, the first item he listed being 750 adobe bricks, for which he paid $10.50. Then, in April of the following year, he chose his site, acquiring a parcel of land some 137 1/2 feet square on what is now the southeast corner of Main and Jefferson streets. This cost him $12.50, plus a $3.25 fee for registering his deed with the provincial authorities.

Thereafter work got actively under way and proceeded at a steady —but by no means rapid—pace for the next three years, the final entries in his account books being made in January 1838. These last included, among other items, $7 for paint and glue, and $8 for papering one of the newly finished rooms.

Of the hundreds of expenses listed during the contruction period, many make curious—and nostalgic—reading to modern home builders. Thus in May of 1835 he paid $11 for eleven wagonloads of white stone, and two months later he bought 12,000 adobe bricks for $180. Nails cost $9 per *arroba* (an *arroba* equalled twenty-five pounds); lumber ranged from $40 to $50 per thousand feet, and shingles for the roof —of which 21,000 were used—came to $210. By September of 1835 building had progressed to the point where the structure was ready to be roofed over, and this was evidently made the occasion for a celebration, for in that month appears this cryptic entry: "Rum for raising the roof, $3."

Then, as now, labor was a major item in building costs, but there again the passage of more than a century has brought drastic changes. Scattered through Larkin's account books we find such entries as these: "April 1835, Paid for 8 men 7 days work making foundation, $38.50;" in June 1836: "Paid Jimmy for one week's work, $5," and in July of that same year: "Paid Smith for finishing room, $17." Unskilled work seems to have been mainly performed by the aboriginals, for there are numerous items reading simply "Paid Indians," with the amounts set down opposite ranging from $1 or $2 to as much as $25 or $30. One entry, dated November 1835, reads: "Gregorio's pay and board for 2 months, $36," which indicates that part of the compensation received by the Indian workers was in the form of food. On other occasions the natives took goods from Larkin's store in lieu of pay, an entry in July 1835 stating: "Paid Indians in trade, $11."

Totaled up, the cost of Larkin's new residence, plus the digging of a well, the building of a bakehouse, an outdoor privy, and the construction of adobe walls enclosing the property, came to slightly less than $5,000. An what did the proud owner get for that, in those days, by no means inconsiderable outlay? On its completion, and for many years thereafter, it was one of the chief architectural ornaments of the town, an impressive, two-story structure with hip roof, solid, three-foot-thick walls, and a spacious second-floor gallery extending across its front and along two sides. Within is a broad central hall running from the street to the inner courtyard, with doors opening into the four ground-floor rooms and a stairway leading up to the sleeping chambers.

In Larkin's day the casa was used both as a residence and place of business, with the owner's living quarters in the rooms to the left as one enters, and those across the hall given over to commercial pursuits. The largest of these latter was known as the Trading Station, and it was there that the rancheros and their womenfolk picked out, in exchange for their hides and tallow, such articles as caught their fancy from Larkin's stock of Boston goods: furniture, dishes and pots and pans, guns and ammunition, clothing and jewelry, and bolts of cloth ranging from bright-colored calicos to somber silks and broadcloth.

Throughout the eventful year 1846, the house was the center about which revolved much of the activity and intrigue incident to the transfer of the province to American ownership. Early that year Consul Larkin received there Lieutenant Archibald Gillespie, who had been sent out from Washington bearing secret messages from President Polk and Secretary of the Navy George Bancroft for him and Captain John C. Frémont. Then, with the arrival in early July of Commodore Sloat's warships and the raising of the American flag above the Custom House at the bay shore, Larkin's casa became the headquarters of the conquerors and remained so until, nearly a year later, they were moved across town to El Cuartel, the adobe put up by the Mexicans in the early 1840s, which stands at the corner of Munras and Webster streets.

During the next several years Larkin continued to live in his Monterey house. Then, soon after the Gold Rush got under way, it having grown obvious that the new settlements on San Francisco Bay offered greater business opportunities than the old Mexican capital, he traded his Monterey property with Jacob P. Leese, who had meantime become a San Francisco merchant, and moved to that fast-growing town. Leese occupied the casa for some years, and after his death, it was acquired by Robert Johnson. Later still it was purchased by Mrs. Harry S. Toulmin, née Alice Larkin, a granddaughter of the man who built it. During the next several years Mrs. Toulmin spent much time and effort restoring it as nearly as possible to its original condition. The result is that the Larkin House today is one of the best preserved and most interesting of the state's historic adobes.

Another of Monterey's historic buildings, within the walls of which were taken the first steps leading to California's admission into the union as a full-fledged state, is Colton Hall, which stands facing Friendly Plaza in the midst of what is now the town's Civic Center. This sturdy, two-story structure, its walls of stone with an outer coating of plaster, was built in the late 1840s, after the taking over of the province by the United States, and on its completion was pronounced "the finest building in all California."

The man responsible for its construction was Walter Colton, Vermont-born writer and editor, who reached California in 1845 on board the flagship of Commodore Stockton's Pacific squadron. Following the American Conquest the next year, he was appointed alcalde, or mayor, of Monterey, a post he continued to occupy until 1849. One of the services for which he is remembered today was his founding, in partnership with Robert Semple, of California's first newspaper, a tiny, four-page weekly called *The Californian*, printed with the meager equipment left behind by the Mexicans and which made its first appearance on August 15, 1846.

As alcalde, Colton early set about making plans for an adequate building in which to conduct the business of the town, and it is said that he himself designed Colton Hall. The result was a pleasing, well-proportioned building, its chief architectural embellishment being a Colonial pediment supported by graceful columns in the center of its façade. At a later period its appearance was seriously marred by the building of outside stairways leading to the second story and passing before the windows of its front. For a time part of the ground floor was used for school purposes, while a commodious assembly hall occupied a major part of the space upstairs.

32. Colton Hall, Monterey. Closely allied with California's beginnings as an American state is this handsome structure. Built in the latter 1840s by Walter Colton, then mayor of the town, it was the meeting place, in September 1849, of delegates from all over the province who drafted a constitution and forwarded it to Washington with a plea for California's admission to the union as a full-fledged state — a hope that became a reality on September 9 of the following year. *Photograph by Lee Blaisdell, Monterey*

PART II: THE COMING OF THE FOREIGNERS

In order to finance its building Colton was forced to resort to a variety of expedients, no funds for that purpose being available in the town's treasury. Tradition has it that the materials were purchased with fines he levied on Monterey's gamblers, drunkards, and other transgressors, plus the scale of town lots, and that much of the labor was performed by inmates of the local calaboose.

Colton Hall was completed in the spring of 1849, and on September 3 of that year there assembled in the big upstairs room forty-eight delegates from all parts of California, who proceeded to draft a constitution for the future state and dispatched it to Washington with an urgent appeal to Congress that it be acted on with a minimum of delay. As a result, the bill admitting California to the union was passed by the Senate on August 13, 1850, by the House on September 7, and received President Fillmore's signature two days later.

For many years thereafter the building was neglected and fell into a deplorable state of disrepair. Early in the present century, however, the property was leased to the state and a comprehensive program of restoration got under way. Today Colton Hall, "the cradle of statehood," is one of the most venerated of California's shrines.

An interesting Monterey landmark dating from before the coming of the Yankees is the old playhouse — the first to be established in California — which stands on the southwest corner of Pacific and Scott streets, two blocks up the hill from the waterfront. This single-story adobe structure was built in 1843 by an ex-seacook named Jack Swan, who had arrived that year on a vessel called the *Soledad* and there opened a combination restaurant, bar, and rooming house.

When, after the American Conquest, several companies of Colonel Jonathan D. Stevenson's regiment of New York Volunteers were sent to Monterey to be mustered out, a group of soldiers, finding time hanging heavily on their hands, organized a theatrical company and, in the spring of 1848, persuaded Jack Swan to permit them to stage a play in the large room of his casa. Their initial offering was entitled *Putnam, or the Lion of '76*, and the receipts from the first performance are said to have totaled $500.

The setting for this production was understandably crude, the stage being a platform elevated only a foot above the floor, while a large wooden door — raised and lowered by means of ropes — served as a curtain, and the footlights were whale-oil lamps and tallow candles. Nonetheless, so welcome was the entertainment provided that the company enjoyed a highly successful season, putting on half a dozen other dramas, their repertory ranging from *Nan, the Good-for-Nothing* to *Romeo and Juliet*.

During the years that followed, the old building was put to a wide variety of uses, being occupied successively by shops, bars, restaurants, and similar establishments, and gradually falling into disrepair. In the early years of the present century the property was purchased by a group of public-spirited Monterey residents and presented to the state, which proceeded to rehabilitate it completely, converting the main structure once more into a pioneer playhouse and assembling in the adjoining wing a collection of early theatrical programs and other historical relics. Today little theater groups both in Monterey and nearby Carmel frequently put on plays there; these are usually revivals of dramas that were popular a century or longer ago.

Yet another well-preserved relic of Monterey's early days is a two-story residence that stands on Decatur Street near the gate of the presidio. Erected in 1855, after wood had replaced adobe bricks as the town's most popular building material, it nonetheless follows closely the architecture of the earlier period, having the characteristic second-floor balcony that projects out over the sidewalk and the usual shed roof, the latter of shingles rather than tiles. It has long been known as the Old Whaling Station, that name having been conferred on it in the early days because it was a favorite stopping place for the crews of Portuguese

33. California's First Theater, Monterey. At the corner of
Pacific and Scott streets, this single-story adobe structure, with
a wooden annex at one end, was built in 1843 and long used
as a rooming house and bar. Here in 1847 a group of soldiers
stationed in the town presented *Putnam, or the Lion of '76*, the
first American play to be seen on California soil.   *Photograph
by Lee Blaisdell, Monterey*

35. Rancho Nipomo, San Luis Obispo County. Built in 1838 by Captain William G. Dana, who had been granted a huge tract of land in the area, this picturesque adobe ranch house was long a favorite stopping place for those traveling up or down the coast. One distinguished guest was John C. Frémont who in December 1846 paused there overnight on his way south to complete the conquest of the province. *Photograph from the Title Insurance & Trust Co., Los Angeles*

34. First Brick House, Monterey. Standing on Decatur Street adjacent to the Old Whaling Station is this sturdy, two-story structure, erected by the Dickinson family in 1847. It is said to be the first brick building put up in California. *Photograph by Lee Blaisdell, Monterey*

whaling vessels, which throughout the latter 1850s and 1860s frequently dropped anchor in Monterey Bay to refit and take on supplies after months-long cruises in Pacific waters.

Early in the present century the old house, which had fallen into a state of disrepair, was taken over by new owners who did a thorough job of restoration, adding the stone wall that encloses its quaint and charming garden. One unique feature of the latter is that its walks are paved with whale vertebrae — a reminder of the long-past day when the little building first received its name.

A few doors down Decatur Street from the Old Whaling Station stands a two-story dwelling built in 1847 by a pioneer resident named Dickinson, and locally celebrated because it was the first Monterey house to be constructed of brick. The bricks, now weathered to an attractive pinkish tone by the suns and rains of more than a century, are said to have been made and fired locally, a pioneer brick-yard having been established nearby earlier that year. In recent times the old building has been occupied by a Spanish family named Garcia, purveyors of tamales, enchiladas, tortillas, and other savory dishes of their homeland — dishes that have been known in Monterey since the first white men settled on the peninsula close to two centuries ago.

On the coast highway some twenty-five miles to the south of San Luis Obispo stands Nipomo, now a picturesque little settlement of less than a thousand inhabitants but in pioneer times an important stopping place for those traveling between the pueblo of Los Angeles in the south and the village of Yerba Buena on San Francisco Bay. For it was long the home of Captain William G. Dana, an energetic New Englander who had reached the coast in 1835, obtained from the Mexican authorities a grant of land comprising some 37,000 acres, and there erected the Casa de Dana, a handsome, thirteen-room adobe that still survives.

A shrewd businessman, as well as a public-spirited citizen, Dana set about making his property one of the most productive of the entire

area, running great herds of cattle on his far-reaching ranges and training his Indian dependents in a variety of useful crafts.   Thus there grew
up about his casa a group of workshops in which were produced such
products as candles, soap, and lard (made from tallow obtained when
his cattle were slaughtered for their hides), flour, sugar, and a fiery
Spanish brandy called *aguardiente*.   But that was not all.   In other shops
were turned out, all by native workmen, wooden furniture, blankets
and other woolen fabrics, and, in the blacksmith shop, farm implements,
tools and a variety of other needed articles.   All these found a ready
market with ranchers and other settlers up and down the coast.   The
raw materials for these primitive manufacturing plants he either grew
on the rancho or obtained — in exchange for hides — from the New
England trading ships that from time to time dropped anchor off a
nearby spot on the coast called Cave Landing.

Besides all this activity, the Nipomo ranch house was, as stated,
a favorite stopping place for travelers, and tradition has it that the
owner extended a welcome to any wayfarer who passed that way, providing food and shelter for him and his mount and asking nothing in
return save the pleasure of his company.   Such openhanded hospitality,
however, was merely in keeping with the custom of the country throughout that free-and-easy period.

Among the noted guests entertained at the Casa de Dana was the
famous pathfinder, John C. Frémont, who stopped there in mid-
December of 1846 while leading an army of 700 men southward to
occupy Santa Barbara and Los Angeles during the taking over of the
province by the United States.   It is said that while Frémont was at
Rancho Nipomo, Captain Dana informed him that a detachment of
Mexican troops were waiting to ambush him and his party at Gaviota
Pass some miles farther to the south.   Dana provided a guide to lead
them through a second pass, thereby avoiding the trap.

Unlike so many other of the early-day California ranch houses,
the Nipomo adobe and the lands surrounding it remained in pos-

session of descendants of the original owner for many years. Following Captain Dana's death in 1858, the casa was continuously occupied by his children and grandchildren until well into the present century. Recently the old house was taken over by the San Luis Obispo Historical Society, and plans at once got under way to restore it to its former condition.

The Rancho Santa Anita, comprising some 13,000 acres, and lying to the east of present-day Pasadena, was in 1841 granted by the Mexican authorities to Hugo Reid, a Scotchman who had settled in California some years earlier, married an Indian woman, and, in 1852, contributed to the *Los Angeles Star* a highly informative series of papers relating to the aborigines of the Los Angeles area. Reid is remembered today chiefly for these Indian papers and for the fact that the picturesque adobe ranch house he built on his Santa Anita property still stands, a historic little structure that is visited by thousands each year.

During the first two decades the rancho passed through a number of hands. Reid lived in his little tile-roofed casa for some years, then sold it and the extensive lands on which it stood to an Englishman named Henry Dalton. The purchase price is said to have amounted to twenty cents per acre — a far cry indeed from the values placed on land in that area a century later. The next recorded owner was William Wolfskill, one of the intrepid band of hunters and trappers who broke new trails throughout the Far West in the 1820s and 1830s. Later Wolfskill turned to agriculture, planted in 1857 the first extensive grove of orange trees to be set out in southern California, and thereby launched the huge citrus industry which has since grown up in that region.

The next owner of the Santa Anita Rancho was an even more colorful figure than William Wolfskill. This was E. J. "Lucky" Baldwin who, having amassed a fortune speculating in stock of the rich silver mines of Nevada's Comstock Lode, purchased the property in the late 1870s. Baldwin had two consuming hobbies, to both of which he gave

36. Hugo Reid Adobe, Santa Anita. The Rancho Santa Anita, comprising some 13,000 acres, was granted to Hugo Reid in 1841 and on it he built this charming, tile-roofed adobe which still stands. The property was later purchased by E. J. "Lucky" Baldwin, colorful Comstock millionaire, who built his own ornate residence nearby and beautified the grounds by setting out thousands of ornamental trees.

Photograph from the Title Insurance & Trust Co., Los Angeles

full rein at Santa Anita. One was the breeding and training of thoroughbred racehorses, and during the next decade numerous animals wearing his colors gave excellent accounts of themselves on the tracks throughout the country.

The result of the second of his hobbies is visible today at numerous spots within the boundaries of the old rancho. For Baldwin had a passion for planting, and during his lifetime he set out large areas of his wooded valley and foothill holdings to orange groves, vineyards, and grainfields. In addition, he laid out extensive gardens about his home, and bordered the roads and driveways of his estate with lines of eucalypti, acacias, palms, and other ornamental trees.

The old Reid house, the first structure to be put up on the property, has been carefully restored and preserved, a sturdy little casa of simple lines and pleasing proportions. It stands on an elevation affording a wide view to the south and east — an area over which once grazed the extensive herds of its original owner, and which today is covered as far as the eye can see by a succession of populous towns and residential areas.

Generally recognized to be the largest and most impressive of the surviving adobe ranch houses in the southern part of the state is Los Cerritos ("Little Hills"), close to the Virginia Country Club grounds and within the boundaries of the present city of Long Beach. It was built in 1844 by Don Juan Temple, one of the group of Yankee youths who, coming out to the west coast in the early days, married a local belle, took out Mexican citizenship, and permanently cast his lot with the residents of that huge and sparsely settled land.

In Temple's case the decision was a wise one, for during the years that followed he prospered in many fields: as pioneer merchant, owner of valuable property in downtown Los Angeles, and as rancher and cattle raiser on a truly epic scale. His rancho, part of an immense, 200,000-acre domain granted in 1784 by the King of Spain to one

37. Patio of the Reid Adobe, Santa Anita. Built in 1839, the little structure stands on a knoll and commands a wide view of the countryside to the south and east. *Photograph from the Title Insurance & Trust Co., Los Angeles*

38. Los Cerritos Ranch House, near Long Beach. Said to
have been the largest and most impressive private residence
put up in southern California during the Spanish-Mexican
period, Los Cerritos (Little Hills) was built in 1844 by Don
Juan Temple, native of Massachusetts, who married one of the
local belles and acquired large holdings in the area. The
above view was taken before the old casa passed to new
owners, who have skillfully restored it to its pristine condition.
Photograph from the Title Insurance & Trust Co., Los Angeles

PART II: THE COMING OF THE FOREIGNERS

Manuel Nieto, Temple acquired as a result of his marriage to Rafaela Cota, a descendant of Nieto. A few years later he bought out the interests of the other heirs and built his impressive casa.

Throughout the next two decades it remained a center of the social life of the area, the scene of rodeos, bullfights, fandangos, barbecues, and other divertissements fancied then by residents of the province. In the mid-1860s, however, a prolonged drought brought that festive era to an end, for many thousands of cattle, horses, and sheep that roamed the hills and valleys of the rancho perished of thirst, and shortly thereafter the property passed into other hands.

Its purchasers were Llewellyn Bixby, a Dr. Thomas, and Benjamin Flint, Bixby acquiring the part of the rancho on which the house stands. For many years after that the big structure either remained vacant or was used as a storehouse or as living quarters for groups of ranch hands, and it gradually fell into disrepair. In recent times, however, Bixby's son, also named Llewellyn, has taken it over, patiently restored it to its original condition and made it again one of the most interesting and historically valuable relics of that long-vanished era.

Today Los Cerritos, both inside and out, faithfully recreates the environment in which wealthy landowners of the province once lived. The main structure, two stories in height, with a broad balcony running the length of its façade, has in the rear two long, low wings enclosing a spacious patio where the owners, now as in the past, spend much of their time during the long, dry summer months. Its thick walls, high, cool rooms, and hand-wrought woodwork make it a veritable museum, a testimonial to the taste and building skill of the early-day artisans who created it.

Some thirty miles north of San Diego and but a short distance from the spot where the Battle of San Pascual, one of the few serious engagements fought during the conquest of the province by the United States forces, stands another extensive and well-preserved example of early-day California domestic architecture. It is situated on the old Rancho Guajome — that is, "the Ranch of the Big Frog" — which was originally a part of the lands belonging to the Mission San Luis Rey. In 1845 it was granted to Andrés and José Manuel, former Mission Indians, who in 1852 sold it to Abel Sterns. The latter had been a prominent, and controversial, figure in southern California affairs during the years prior to the conquest of the province by the Yankees.

Soon after Sterns acquired the property he presented it as a wedding gift to a sister-in-law, Ysidori Bandini, upon her marriage to Cave J. Couts, an American resident of the new state. It was by them that the picturesque casa and its surrounding barns, corrals, and servants' quarters were built. The casa itself, an excellent example of the more pretentious type of early California ranch houses, is a one-story adobe laid out in the form of a U, with the doors of the various rooms opening onto an inner patio planted to oranges and other semi-tropical trees, in the center of which stands a graceful fountain.

Of particular interest to visitors nowadays are the outlying buildings, for at all but a few of the surviving ranch houses of that period these attendant structures have long since disappeared. At Rancho Guajome these include, besides the barns, stables, and other buildings mentioned above, a quaint little chapel in which the family and the sheepherders, farmhands, and other retainers worshipped.

During the early years following the taking over of the province by the United States, a gradual change took place in the prevailing style of architecture at Monterey, Santa Barbara, Los Angeles, San Diego, and elsewhere. The white walls and red tile roofs long characteristic of these Spanish provincial towns had by the end of the first decade seen an admixture of many sorts of other structures: austere New England cottages, Pennsylvania farmhouses, Southern colonial manors, plus brick or stone or wooden residences of many sorts and sizes.

39. Patio of the Guajome Ranch House, near San Diego. One of the last of the early-day adobes — it was built in the 1850s, after California had become an American state — it is nonetheless typical of the more pretentious residences of Spanish and Mexican days, its many rooms opening on an inner patio. *Photograph from the Title Insurance & Trust Co., Los Angeles*

The majority of these have long since disappeared, victims of a century's wear and tear or, if the town's business district chanced to spread in their direction, torn down to make way for factory, store, or office building. Of the few such still standing, one of the most interesting is the Whaley House at the northeast corner of San Diego Avenue and Harney Street in San Diego's Old Town. Built in 1856 by Thomas Whaley, a native of Brooklyn, New York, it was regarded on its completion as one of the most elegant homes in the new state.

The structure, which is still owned by descendants of its original builder, is in excellent condition, showing few signs of age despite the century it has been standing. This is due not only to the care it has received but equally to the quality of the materials and workmanship that went into its construction. Its outer walls are of brick, made in a kiln set up by Whaley on the premises, and are finished in a plaster composed of ground seashells. All the wood used, save only the flooring, is of white cedar. This was brought round the Horn from the Atlantic Coast, as were also the hardware used throughout and the furniture, much of which is still in use.

40. Whaley House, San Diego. Its walls of bricks made in a kiln set up on the property in 1856, and its wood and hardware brought out from the east coast on board the round-the-Horn clipper ships, this sturdy building has sheltered five generations of Whaleys, descendants of its builder, Thomas Whaley. For a time during the early days its ground floor was occupied by the San Diego County Courthouse. *Photograph from the Union Title Insurance & Trust Co., San Diego*

PART

III

THE ARGONAUTS

With the discovery of particles of gold in the millrace of Captain Sutter's sawmill in the Sierra foothills, California entered into a new and, of course, quite different phase of its evolution. With hordes of miners converging on the remote land from every corner of the globe, the leisurely, pastoral life its inhabitants had long known speedily passed into history. Newcomers by the thousands flowed into the country each month during the next several years, some coming by water and others via one or another of the overland trails, overrunning such primitive settlements as existed on the seacoast and in the interior, and pushing on to the succession of diggings that extended from Mariposa northward to Mount Shasta and beyond, a distance of close to 300 miles.

Throughout the early days of the rush, housing was a lightly regarded detail. At San Francisco the newly landed paused only long enough to get their goods ashore and make ready to push on to the goldfields, meantime living in tents or in such rough board shacks as could be hastily thrown up. In the diggings the living quarters of the first comers were no more elaborate, with many sleeping and cooking in the open or putting up rude shelters of logs or stone roofed over with pine boughs.

It was not long, however, before California saw the beginnings of what has since become known as Gold Rush architecture. In the cities and towns a succession of destructive fires led to the construction of scores of stone and brick buildings to house the stores, banks, bars, and other business establishments. While by far the greater number of these have long since disappeared, victims of the march of progress, those few that remain possess a rare charm in the eyes of the historically minded. Well built, they have for the most part admirably withstood the passage of the years, their plain and forthright façades, devoid of superfluous ornamentation, and their characteristic iron shutters before doors and windows forming a pleasant contrast to the ornate, begabled structures put up by a later generation.

It is in the gold towns of the Sierra foothills that the architecture of the 1850s can today be seen at its best. For while examples of these venerable relics are still to be found in San Francisco, Sacramento, Los Angeles, and other coast and valley cities, the majority have either been given new fronts, or otherwise modernized, or are overshadowed and dwarfed by adjacent tall buildings. In certain of the Mother Lode towns, among them Columbia, Angels Camp, and Downieville, they have been spared that fate. Mainly because with the decline of mining in the adjacent streams and gulches the towns' brief heyday came to a permanent close, many of their buildings have stood untenanted and undisturbed ever since. Thus visitors now have little difficulty visualizing the scene as it appeared during the height of the boom a century and more ago, with hordes of miners crowding the board sidewalks, streaming into the stores and bars and gaming rooms and, their brief contacts with urban life at an end, setting off again for their lonely claims in the back country.

PART III: THE ARGONAUTS

Fortunately, Columbia, one of the best preserved of the gold towns, has been acquired by the state as a historical shrine, and for some years work has been in progress restoring it as nearly as possible to its condition in the days when it was known as "The Gem of the Southern Mines." Today the buildings lining its curving, tree-shaded main street, one- and two-story structures with their wooden balconies extending over the sidewalks, constitute a re-creation of a past epoch and a long-vanished way of life that in its field has an importance — and interest — comparable to that of the far-better-known restorations of buildings dating from colonial days at Williamsburg, Virginia.

While early business houses are fairly numerous, few examples of domestic architecture dating from the 1850s are to be found in Columbia or other gold towns, and for obvious reasons. Virtually none of the early residents planned to remain there permanently, the aim of the great majority being to wrest a quick fortune from the placers, or from trading with the miners, and to hurry back to their homes on the east coast or elsewhere. The consequence was that the typical residence of the period was a makeshift affair, usually a small, unpretentious frame structure containing but one or two rooms and so flimsily constructed that few of them have survived the passage of the years.

Among the more ostentatious buildings in the gold towns were the hotels, of which a number still stand. One of the most picturesque of these is the Eureka House (now called the Saint George) at the moldering town of Volcano in the heart of the Mother Lode, some ten miles to the northeast of Jackson. The town itself, so named because its first settlers fancied that its location, walled in by a circle of steep hills, resembled a crater, was among the richest of the area, once boasting a population of above 5,000. An indication of the productiveness of its mines may be gained by the fact that when the Adams Express Company opened its office there in 1852 — in a stone building that still stands — queues of miners daily formed before all four entrances to ship

41. Mother Lode Hotel. High in the foothills to the south-east of Sacramento is the village of Volcano, once the center of a rich mining district. Among many relics of its brief boom that still stand is this picturesque, three-story hotel dating from the early 1850s and still in use. *Photograph by Harry W. Abrahams, San Francisco*

42. Pioneer Hotel, Dutch Flat. One of the most impressive
buildings in the block-long business section of the foothill town
of Dutch Flat is this three-story hotel, a popular stopping
place for transmontane travelers before the building of the
railroad. Many of its original furnishings are still in use,
including an ornate mirror that once hung behind its bar, and
a group of old ledgers in which are entered the amounts of
gold taken from the diggings of the area.   *Photograph by*
V. Covert Martin, Stockton

their gold home. Today the town has a population of fewer than 200.

Volcano's Eureka House, a sturdy, three-story hostelry, its façade ornamented by broad galleries opening out from rooms on the second and third stories, has well withstood the passage of the years. This can be accounted for mainly by the fact that it has been continuously occupied from the day of its completion. Today it is a favorite stopping place for parties making a tour of the southern mines, who find in its big, high-ceilinged rooms, its broad corridors, and its quaint barroom, all virtually unchanged from the day of its opening, the authentic atmosphere of a long-past era.

Some twenty-five miles to the south of Downieville, on the route of the old heavily traveled trans-Sierra wagon road via Donner Pass, stands the historic village of Dutch Flat, its single main street once crowded with stagecoaches and heavily loaded freight wagons carrying passengers and goods over the summit. Still existing is the charming old Dutch Flat hotel, which during the 1850s and early 1860s was nightly crowded to capacity, it being one of the regular stopping places of the east- and west-bound overland stages. Today the building, its balconies shaded by a line of venerable poplar trees, contains numerous relics of the days of its glory. These include old registers bearing the names of scores of distinguished guests, together with an ornate mirror that once occupied the wall behind its bar, and tattered record books listing the amounts of gold deposited there for safekeeping by miners during the early days of the camp.

Columbia contains two old-time hostelries, the Fallon House and the City Hotel. Both are two-story structures, their walls of brick, and with the doors and windows on the street level protected by iron shutters that, closed for a few hours each night, were folded back the rest of the time. Because of the solidity of their construction, plus the fact that after its first years of hectic activity, the town was virtually deserted for many years, both buildings are but little changed from the day they were first put up.

PART III: THE ARGONAUTS

In the beginning the Mother Lode towns were constructed almost entirely of wood, for everywhere in the Sierra foothills forests were close at hand and primitive sawmills were operating throughout the region by the early 1850s. It was not until a succession of disastrous fires consumed many of the settlements — Sonora had three such visitations between 1849 and 1853, Nevada City had four from 1851 to 1863, and others fared almost as badly — that less inflammable building materials came into general use. In their determination to guard against fires, the early residents built sturdily and well, not only constructing the outer walls of their stores, offices, and other establishments of masonry, but fitting the doors and windows with heavy iron shutters that could be closed should fire threaten. As an added protection, the roofs of many of these old structures were composed of sheets of metal, or, if of wood, were covered to a depth of several inches with a layer of sand.

While the passage of so many years has tended to make these venerable structures look much alike at first glance, on closer examination certain marked differences can be observed, both in their design and in the materials used. Some of these differences stem from the racial strains that were predominant in the different communities. Thus in the towns near the southern end of the Lode, notably at Hornitos and adjacent camps, where the miners were mostly of Mexican origin, virtually every surviving house has walls of adobe. Farther to the north, where the Yankees were in the majority, stone and bricks were the favored building materials.

Among the least changed of the early mining towns is Weaverville, the county seat of Trinity County, which lies in the rugged, heavily wooded section of the Coast Range, some fifty miles to the northwest of Redding. Founded by a miner named John Weaver, who in 1849 made a rich strike there, during the next several years it was the center of one of the most active gold regions of the state, with scores of camps springing up along the banks of its swift-flowing streams.

Virtually all these outlying settlements have long since disappeared, for as the placer claims were one by one exhausted, their owners abandoned them and hurried off in quest of more profitable diggings. Weaverville, which from the beginning had been the chief trading and social center of the area, likewise went into a profound decline, its population shrinking from a top of 3,000 — which was reached in 1852 — to less than a tenth that number a decade later. Today the picturesque old town, its main street lined with ancient one- and two-story buildings of brick or stone, and shaded by big, century-old locust trees, possesses a somnolent charm that never fails to captivate those visitors who are at all interested in the romance and drama of gold rush days.

That Weaverville, far more than most of Californis's gold towns, has retained down to the present so many relics of its brief heyday is due to three circumstances. First, destructive fires were so frequent during 1850 and 1851 that after the last visitation the merchants and other businessmen abandoned wood and rebuilt with other materials; consequently, many of the old structures still stand, to all appearances as sound as the day they were put up. Second, because the town lies in the midst of one of the most sparsely populated parts of the state, a region of rugged hills and winding, steep-walled canyons, it has not, like so many other early gold camps, grown into a modern town serving the needs of thickly settled farming, dairying, or fruit-growing communities. Finally, it is well off the main-traveled highways and, having few tourists, lacks the assemblage of motels, service stations, drive-in restaurants, and garages that in recent years have so altered the appearance of virtually all the Mother Lode towns.

However, those who go to the trouble of seeking out this picturesque small settlement feel themselves amply repaid. For the twin rows of prim little business structures that line its main street are, in nearly every instance, authentic relics of the days of gold. It is easy to picture the town as it was a century and more ago, when at every hour of the day and night the sidewalks were jammed, when music blared

43. Spiral Stairway, Weaverville: One of the least changed of California's gold towns is Weaverville, situated in the Coast Range Mountains some thirty miles to the northwest of Red-ding. Several of its 100-year-old brick buildings still retain graceful circular stairways leading upward from the sidewalk to their second-floor balconies. *Photograph by Harry W. Abrahams, San Francisco*

from a dozen bars and dancehalls, and its now all but deserted street was crowded with a motley assemblage of vehicles, ranging from the carts and buggies of properous mine-owners, on through stagecoaches and strings of heavily laden pack animals, to great lumbering freight wagons drawn by as many as ten horses or mules.

A unique architectural feature of the town, and one that rarely fails to arouse the curiosity of visitors, is the graceful spiral stairway in front of several of the old buildings, by means of which their second floors could be reached without entering the buildings themselves. Still in use, these handsome stairs curve upward from the outer edge of the sidewalk to the covered second-floor balconies, exhibiting a symmetry of design that bespeaks the skill and taste of their builders, and lending a touch of elegance to the sturdy old structures they adorn.

Of the scores of Weaverville buildings dating from the early 1850s, three of the most interesting architecturally are the Native Sons and the Odd Fellows halls — each of which has a spiral stairway — and the Chinese Joss House. The latter is an ornate little temple, in the dim, candle-lit interior of which are still preserved antique tapestries, brass incense burners, and carved teakwood figures brought from the Flowery Kingdom and installed there well over eighty years ago.

Some twenty-five miles to the southeast of Weaverville, and lining both sides of the highway leading to Redding, stands the melancholy remains of what was once one of the most populous — and prosperous — of northern California's gold towns. This is Shasta City, today little more than a two-blocks-long assemblage of crumbling brick and stone buildings, for the most part roofless, their doors and windows missing, and with manzanitas, chaparral, and other shrubs — and in some places sizable trees — growing out of the rubble-strewn areas that were once their interiors.

During its heyday Shasta was the chief trading center of the rich Trinity River mining district, a region of rugged, thickly forested mountains and canyons, from the swift-flowing streams of which gold in impressive quantities was mined. There were periods during 1852 and 1853 when the shipments of dust from Shasta City alone averaged more than $10,000 a week.

The camp, known originally as Reading Spring, was founded early in 1849, and by the fall of that year had several hundred inhabitants, all living in tents. The rush to the Trinity River diggings continued throughout the next year, and the next, and Shasta grew by leaps and bounds, the tents being replaced first by wooden buildings and then, following several destructive fires, by the sturdy, fireproof structures the walls of which may be seen today.

Shasta's decline was, however, almost as rapid as its rise. For as the placer claims of the back country were one by one worked out and the miners drifted elsewhere, each year a growing number of the town's merchants, bankers, innkeepers, and others were obliged to close their doors. The little community was already beginning to take on the aspect of a ghost town when, in the early 1870s, came the final blow: the decision on the part of the builders of the California-Oregon Railroad to by-pass the settlement and lay its tracks some six miles farther to the east. In 1888 the county seat of Shasta County, which had been located at Shasta City since the county was created in 1851, was moved to Redding, and the little gold town sank still further into insignificance.

Today but little remains save the twin lines of crumbling masonry walls, the vacant windows of which look out blankly on what was once a thoroughfare crowded with a jostling throng from curb to curb at every hour of the day and night. Only two or three of the picturesque old structures have been preserved. One is the Masonic Temple, a two-story brick building put up in 1853, the ground floor of which was occupied by Norton & Tucker, merchants, and with a hall above in which met what is said to have been the first Masonic lodge to be established in California, the charter of which — still preserved in a vault on the premises — was brought out from Missouri by Peter Lassen in 1850. At the far end of the street stands the venerable store put up by Bull, Baker & Company in the early 1850s, and which now houses not only the post office and a little stock of merchandise but a collection of relics of the early days: gold scales, daggers, derringers, and other weapons, gambling paraphernalia, daguerreotypes, and the like.

Standing on a little hill at the edge of the town is the only surviving residence dating from pioneer days. This is a two-story frame house built in 1851 and long the home of Dr. Ben Shurtleff, once mayor of the settlement and for many years its leading physician. The old building is now falling into ruin; nonetheless it still bears evidences of the elegancies in design and finish that made it one of the show-places of the settlement throughout the early days.

Proceeding southward from Shasta City, one comes to the northern end of the Mother Lode and the town of Grass Valley, on one of the quiet, tree-lined streets of which stands a little frame cottage that a century ago was known throughout the length and breadth of California. Its widespread fame — or perhaps notoriety would be a more accurate word — was not due to anything unusual about its appearance, for all accounts agree that in its original state, before a second story was added by a later owner, it was a modest structure not noticeably different from a score of others in the picturesque foothill town.

What, then, it might be asked, was the reason for its renown, a renown that even today draws throngs of the curious to the spot, to troop through its cluttered downstairs rooms and stroll among the flower beds and huge poplar trees of its old-fashioned garden? The answer is that during much of the years 1853 and 1854 it was the abode of one of the most widely known and avidly discussed young women ever to appear on the Western frontier. This was none other than Lola Montez, dancer and actress of no more than average ability, who some six years earlier had attracted international attention as the mistress of King Louis I of Bavaria, a circumstance that had ultimately cost that elderly monarch his throne.

44. Keeler House, Grass Valley. One of many picturesque residences dating from the 1850s or earlier that line the streets of this quiet Mother Lode town is this two-story frame dwelling that was once the home of a pioneer merchant named Keeler. *Photograph by Tyler's Studio, Grass Valley*

45. Brick House, Nevada City. Long known to the natives as "The Castle," this ornate little residence with its steep-pitched roof and pointed windows has well withstood the vicissitudes of more than a century. Standing high on the side of Deer Creek Canyon, its windows overlook the town.
Photograph by Prentiss, Nevada City

PART III: THE ARGONAUTS

The beautiful and wily Lola, whose true name was Eliza Gilbert, had come West in 1852 after a series of appearances in New York and other cities of the Atlantic seaboard, and for some weeks had played to crowded houses in San Francisco. Then, having married Patrick Hull, editor of one of the local newspapers, she had set off on a tour of the towns and camps of the interior. Following a quarrel at Sacramento the newly wed couple had parted, Hull returning to the bay city and Lola making her way up into the hills to Grass Valley.

There in the little house at the corner of Mill and Walsh streets she established what she termed a *salon*, at which gathered nightly the elite of the small community. One of the regular attendants was Alonzo Delano, a widely known journalist who wrote under the name of "Old Block." Lola's gracious hospitality, her Paris gowns, and her pet bear — which she is said to have led by a chain on her strolls about the town — quickly made her a favorite throughout the northern Mother Lode. During her stay she befriended the six-year-old daughter of a boardinghouse keeper who lived nearby, taught her a few simple songs and dance steps, and thus launched the child-actress Lotta Crabtree on what was to prove a distinguished career.

Upon leaving her mountain retreat, Lola led a theatrical troupe on a tour of Australia, played again briefly in San Francisco, and then returned to the Atlantic coast. She died at Boston in 1861, at the early age of forty-three.

Clinging to the steep-sided slopes of Deer Creek Canyon, on the floor of which stands the town of Nevada City, are a number of picturesque miners' houses dating from the 1850s. All of these are solidly built and some indeed possess a degree of elegance, for Nevada City, together with its neighboring town of Grass Valley, lay in the midst of one of the choicest mining districts of the entire Mother Lode. Following the uncovering of rich placer claims in the summer of 1850, it was no uncommon thing for certain lucky miners to pan out a quart of

46. Stewart Mansion, Nevada City. This was the home of a young New Yorker named William M. Stewart, who arrived in the town in 1852, studied law in the office of a local attorney, and, shortly after being admitted to the bar, was appointed district attorney of Nevada County. Later Stewart joined the rush over the Sierra to the newly opened silver mines at Virginia City and in 1865 he was elected United States Senator from Nevada. *Photograph by Prentiss, Nevada City*

47. Assay Office, Nevada City. Of the group of venerable, iron-shuttered buildings fronting on Nevada City's Commercial Street, one of the most interesting is the Assay Office, which was first opened in 1853 and has been in continuous operation ever since. It was here, in the spring of 1859, that the first ores from Nevada's new silver mines were brought for assay, the findings of which set off the great rush to the Comstock Lode. *Photograph by Prentiss, Nevada City*

nuggets and gold dust in a single day. This, at the going rate of $12 per ounce, amounted to between $5,000 and $6,000.

One of the most interesting of the surviving relics of that high-riding period is a steep-roofed brick house perched atop one of the hills and long known to the townspeople as The Castle. The precise date of its building is uncertain, some authorities placing it as early as 1852 and others up to a half-dozen years later. It is known, however, that it was standing in 1859, for in that year it was occupied by William M. Stewart, who was soon to become an important figure in the affairs of the Nevada Comstock Lode and to top off his career by a term as United States Senator from that state. It was, in fact, at the Assay Office on the flat below that samples of the Comstock ores were first tested and found to be so rich in silver as to set in motion a mightly eastward rush across the Sierra in the fall of 1859.

The Castle has well withstood the wear and tear of the years. The peaked windows of its upper story give the structure an architectural distinction unique among Mother Lode residences dating from the 1850s. The wooden porch that projects from two sides, and which commands a view of the rugged, tree-covered countryside, is also structurally sound after a lapse of more than nine decades — a tribute alike to the materials and craftsmanship employed by the early-day artisans, and to the care of later tenants.

A movement has recently been launched by the townspeople to acquire the property, to restore the old building to its original condition and fill its quaint, high-ceilinged rooms with furniture, lithographs, letters, newspapers and other documents dating from the period when Nevada City was the business, financial, and recreational center for one of California's richest mining districts.

Another of the buildings dating from gold rush days that still stands in Nevada City, and one of the most interesting, is the Assay Office mentioned above. This two-story stone structure, with iron shutters before

48. Firehouse, Nevada City.   In all the Mother Lode settlements fire was an ever-present menace and the buildings that housed the hand-operated pumps and other equipment were often among the most impressive in the towns.   In Nevada City this sturdy structure, erected in the early 1860s, still stands.   *Photograph by Prentiss, Nevada City*

its doors and windows, has been in continuous use as an assay office since it was built well over a century ago. For mining has remained a major industry in that area from 1849 down to the present, and the assaying of ores to learn their content of precious metals has long been the determining factor in deciding whether or not a claim can be profitably worked. One memorable day in 1859 there appeared at the Assay Office a prospector from the far side of the Sierra, who laid on the counter some pieces of slate-colored rock he had picked up on the slope of Sun Mountain in Nevada Territory. A few simple tests revealed that the samples were silver ore of unprecedented richness. Thus was set in motion a concerted rush across the mountains to the Comstock Lode, the mines of which were during the next two decades to add hundreds of millions of dollars to the nation's wealth.

Fire was an ever-present menace in all the Sierra gold towns throughout the earliest days, for then virtually all buildings were of wood and unless a blaze could be promptly extinguished it spread with lightning speed, often reducing whole blocks to ruin before burning itself out. The consequence was that one of the first civic enterprises launched by the merchants, innkeepers, and other businessmen was the recruiting of a fire brigade and the purchase of equipment: namely, a hosecart, buckets, ladders, and a hand-operated pump.

Throughout the 1850s and 1860s members of these organizations were all volunteers, young men of standing in their communities who bound themselves to respond to the tolling of the fire bell at any hour of the day or night. To ally themselves with such groups was considered not only a civic duty but an honor, one that conferred on members a certain prestige. For the fire laddies were looked on as belonging to the social elect; their annual balls were gala affairs, and no parade was complete without their presence, resplendent in red shirts and patent leather helmets, marching near the head of the column and drawing their hosecart and pump, the brass fittings of the latter glistening in the sun.

49. National Hotel, Nevada City. Typical of the Mother Lode hostelries of the 1850s and later is the three-story National Hotel at Nevada City, complete with sidewalk balcony extending the length of its façade. Because in the early days one of the heavily traveled transmontane roads passed through the town, a succession of stages and great, lumbering freight wagons paused there at all hours of the day and night.
Photograph by Prentiss, Nevada City

50. Iron Shutters, Nevada City. Because fires were frequent
in the early gold towns, brick and stone presently became the
most widely used building materials, particularly in the business sections. As an added protection, iron shutters were
installed before the doors and windows, which could be closed
should danger threaten. *Photograph by Prentiss, Nevada City*

PART III: THE ARGONAUTS

The firehouses where this equipment was held in readiness were likely to be among the chief architectural embellishments of the gold towns, standing as they did near the center of the business districts and surmounted by towers in which hung the fire bells. Usually they were two stories high, their upper floors serving as clubrooms, complete with libraries and card tables, where members and their guests gathered evenings.

By far the greater number of these ornate little structures have long since disappeared, having shared the fate of most of the other buildings in the crumbling towns. A few, however, have escaped. One of the most picturesque of these is to be seen at Nevada City. Built in the early 1860s, the two-story frame firehouse is a striking example of the complex architecture then in vogue, its street frontage ornamented by a series of balconies rising to a lofty tower, the whole heavily encrusted with the profusion of balustrades and other decorations admired by the Victorians.

The original equipment the little building once sheltered — most of which came round the Horn in the clipper ships of the period — has for the most part been scattered and lost. However, the venerable bell, close to a century old, still hangs in the tower and is ceremoniously rung on July 4 and other gala occasions.

Long an object of curiosity to those visiting the towns and abandoned diggings of the Mother·Lode is a handsome, three-story structure, built in an architectural style reminiscent of the plantation houses of the Old South, which stands in a grove of venerable oaks and locusts near the village of Pilot Hill, on the road between Auburn and Coloma.

This is the Bayley House, built in 1862 by Alexander Bayley, a native of Vermont who reached California in 1849 aboard the *Edward Everett*, which had sailed from Boston early that year carrying a capacity load of Argonauts, many of whom later became prominent in the annals of the state. Bayley settled at Pilot Hill where, from 1851 to 1861, he owned and operated a hotel known as the Oak Valley House. When that building was destroyed in one of the frequent mining town fires, he built beside the road a short distance north of Pilot Hill the impressive structure that still stands and which has ever since been known as the Bayley House.

From the day of its completion, and for many years thereafter, it was one of the largest and most admired buildings on the entire Mother Lode. Three stories high, its outer walls of brick, and with its front ornamented by a series of tall, graceful columns supporting a second-floor gallery, it stood in the midst of a formal, terraced garden unlike any to be seen for many miles about.

The reason why Bayley erected so elaborate a house in that out-of-the-way spot can be explained by the fact that the western half of the first transcontinental railroad was then getting under way and Bayley had been assured that on their passage through the foothills its rails would pass close by, thus providing a steady flow of patrons to his fine new hotel. Instead, when actually built, the road followed a quite different route, passing through Auburn, some ten miles farther north and leaving the Bayley House permanently bereft of guests.

Thereafter the house stood vacant for many years, while the paint peeled from its columns and the flowers and shrubs of its garden were engulfed by the native vegetation. The house itself, however, had been strongly built and withstood the wear and tear of the years in admirable fashion. Recently the venerable old landmark came into the possession of new owners who, by the exercise of much care and skill, have restored both house and grounds to their original condition, making it one of the most charming — and historically interesting — residences to be seen anywhere on the Sierra foothills.

In Eldorado County, a dozen miles to the east of Auburn and some 1,000 feet higher into the mountains, lies picturesque little Georgetown, once one of the liveliest spots of the northern Mother Lode but now, like so many other settlements of the area, a quiet, sleepy village with a

51. Bayley House, Pilot Hill. One of the handsomest structures in the entire Mother Lode, this three-story brick mansion
was long known as "Bayley's Folly," its owner Alexander
Bayley, having built it as an inn in the early 1860s in the
belief that the transcontinental railroad would pass that way.
Instead, a route farther to the north was selected and the
house, together with its extensive formal gardens, long stood
idle.   *Photograph from Sutter's Fort Museum, Sacramento*

population numbering less than a tenth of what it was during its prime. Present-day visitors who wander down the board sidewalks of its main street, bordered by twin lines of ancient locust trees, find many of its century-old stone and brick buildings standing forlorn and vacant, while of the hundreds of little wooden structures that formerly stood in its residential district only a scattering few remain.

.The town, whose civic-minded residents once proudly termed it "the pride of the mountains," has had a checkered history. The original settlement, known as Growlersburg, lay at the bottom of a nearby canyon, where it was founded by a group of Oregonians who arrived in the area in 1849. Three years later, however, a fire leveled the entire camp and, instead of rebuilding on the same spot, a new site was selected on the top of a ridge between the Middle and South Forks of the American River. The spot chosen was in a grove of tall sugar pines; there a 100-foot-wide main street was laid out and the merchants of the old settlement put up substantial new buildings. The former name of Growlersburg was discarded as inappropriate to the new town and it was rechristened Georgetown in honor of George Phipps, leader of the original band of settlers.

During the next few years the settlement flourished; it was the main trading center for scores of camps then active in the vicinity, and boasted, in addition to its quota of stores, bars, hotels, and other mercantile establishments, a school, a church, a theater, and three halls that served as meeting places respectively for the Masons, the Odd Fellows, and the Sons of Temperance. A few of these old structures remain today, some vacant and falling to ruin, others still in use and kept in reasonable repair.

Of the early Georgetown residences that have survived, the most picturesque is the Knox House, which stands on the main street opposite the Odd Fellows' Hall. This well-proportioned, two-story frame dwelling, its front partially screened from passersby by a group of gnarled fruit trees, was erected in the mid-1860s by Shannon Knox, an early resident whose original house, built of hand-hewn logs, once stood on the site.

The present house, for all its ninety years, is still in sound condition, having been continuously occupied since the day of its completion, during most of that period by descendants of its first owner. Its most notable architectural feature is the broad porch that extends across the front. This is two stories high, the second floor of which, opening out from the upstairs bedrooms, has a prim and graceful wooden balustrade.

The throngs who were drawn to the goldfields in 1849 — and later — not only established scores of camps and towns in the diggings themselves; they were responsible, too, for the building of numerous inns, stables, and other buildings at various spots along the main-traveled routes from the valley, where those journeying to and from the mines could find food or shelter for man and beast.

With the passage of the years by far the majority of these wayside stopping places were swept away. In many cases their very locations have been forgotten, a mention of their names awakening no glimmer of recollection in the memory of the oldest inhabitants of the districts where they once stood.

One of the few such structures to have survived is a big, two-story frame building known as the John Reddick House, which stands at a spot in the valley called Fourth Crossing, on the once heavily traveled road between Stockton and the foothill town of Murphy's Diggings. In the early days a considerable village sprang up at Fourth Crossing — a post office was established there in the 1850s — but the Reddick House is one of the few buildings still standing. The settlement is said to have received its name because it was located on the fourth stream those passing that way had to cross after leaving Stockton.

Fronting on the wide, tree-bordered streets of Marysville, the pleasant valley town that lies some forty miles to the north of Sacramento, are two residences of far more than average interest, both dating from the days of the gold rush. One, known locally as the Field House,

52: John Reddick House, Fourth Crossing. In the Sierra foothills between Angel's Camp and San Andreas stands this two-story frame building, originally the home of a pioneer miner named John Reddick. Later the structure was converted into a hotel and bar, the wing to the right being added at that time. It is supposed to have been in the vicinity of Fourth Crossing that Bret Harte gained his limited experience as a panner of gold.   *Photograph by V. Covert Martin, Stockton*

53. Field House, Marysville. This quaint little brick dwelling, standing at 630 D Street and now walled in by larger buildings, is locally noted as the home of Stephen J. Field, a young New York lawyer who arrived in 1849, became the town's first mayor, and, in 1863, was appointed by President Lincoln a justice of the United States Supreme Court, a post he continued to hold for thirty-four years. *Photograph by Albrecht & Lowe, Marysville*

stands at 630 D Street, a little brick house put up in the early 1850s and ever since occupied as a private dwelling. Its original owner was Stephen J. Field, a 34-year-old attorney who reached the spot in the fall of 1849 and only three days after his arrival was elected mayor of the settlement. Tradition has it that he was elevated to this office mainly because he had purchased some 200 lots in the newly laid-out townsite.

Because Marysville stood at the head of navigation on the Feather River, it speedily became the leading trading and transportation center for the score or more of booming mining communities that lay to the east and north. Goods intended for these points were brought up from San Francisco on the little stern-wheel steamers of the period and sent on to their destinations by pack trains or lumbering freight wagons. So great was this traffic that by 1854 no less than twenty freighting companies were operating out of the town, their equipment consisting of 400 wagons drawn by 4,000 horses and mules.

The owner of the picturesque D Street residence was destined to go on to a distinguished career. In 1850 Field was elected to the state legislature, and in 1857 to the state supreme court, becoming chief justice two years later. Then, in 1863, President Lincoln appointed him to the United States Supreme Court, on which august body he served for a period of more than a third of a century, resigning in 1897 when he reached the age of eighty-one. He died two years later.

Another of Marysville's historic residences is that of José M. Ramirez, also one of the town's first settlers, whose stone and wood dwelling stands at 220 Fifth Street between C and D. Its ground floor walls made of stone blocks and its upper story of wood, the big, rambling building has long been known to the townspeople as "The Castle" — a name suggested by the fact that its vine-covered exterior is replete with gables and outside stairways and pierced by tall, pointed windows in the Gothic manner.

54. Ramirez House, Marysville. Known locally as "The Castle," this ornate structure stands at 220 Fifth Street, its vine-covered exterior, outside stairway, and Gothic windows rarely failing to capture the attention of passersby. Built in the early 1850s, it was the home of José M. Ramirez, prominent resident of the early town.   *Photograph by Albrecht & Lowe, Marysville*

55. Mariposa County Courthouse, Mariposa. This handsome old building dates from 1854, and is still in use. Within the courtroom the spectators' benches and judge's desk are those originally installed more than a century ago. *Photograph from the California Historical Society, San Francisco*

PART III: THE ARGONAUTS

In the quaint town of Mariposa, situated in the Sierra foothills at the southern end of the Mother Lode, stands a building that for more than a century has continuously served the purpose for which it was built. This is the courthouse, put up in 1854 when the county seat of Mariposa County — one of the twenty-seven into which the state was originally divided — was transferred there from nearby Agua Fria.

Standing apart from the other buildings of the town and surrounded by a little grove of pines and other indigenous trees and shrubs, the forthright, two-story structure has an austerity of outline that suggests the town halls of early New England villages. This impression is furthered by the little square clock tower that surmounts its roof, and which contains the same mechanism that has been telling time to the residents since Civil War days.

Certain features of the construction of the venerable courthouse throw light on the methods used by the early builders in Mariposa and other Mother Lode towns. For the spot was then a remote and isolated one; many of the materials available in more settled communities were not to be had, and the artisans had of necessity to improvise substitutes. How well they succeeded may be judged by the fact that today, more than a hundred years later, the structure is to all appearances as sound as the day it was completed. It has been said that every piece of lumber that went into its building was hand sawed from trees that grew in the neighborhood, including not only the clapboard sheathing of its outer walls and the meticulously wrought interior finish, but the heavy timbers that comprise its frame. There being no spikes available, the rafters, joists, and other timbers were joined by fitting their ends together by what is known as the mortise-and-tenon method. They were then secured by wooden pegs.

To modern visitors, one of the most interesting features of the old building is its courtroom, the judge's bench and seating arrangements of which have remained unchanged since the earliest days and where

133

today justice is dispensed in precisely the same surroundings as it was a century ago.

The townspeople are justly proud of their historic old building — said to be the oldest courthouse in the state still in use — and have vigorously opposed suggestions that it be replaced by a more modern and convenient structure. Instead it has been kept in excellent repair and there is every likelihood that it will continue to serve for many years to come. One modern feature has, however, been installed; namely, a fireproof vault, in which are kept not only the current records of the county but the time-yellowed files of the town's first newspapers and numerous other documents dating from its earliest days.

PART

IV

THE AGE OF THE MOGULS

During the first few years that followed James Marshall's momentous discovery in the Coloma millrace, gold mining became and remained California's chief industry. It was, of course, the lure of the precious metal that drew tens of thousands to these then remote shores, that caused scores of towns and camps to spring up beside the foothill streams or deep in the mountain canyons from Mariposa north to the Oregon border, that caused the founding of populous supply towns at Sacramento, Stockton, and other points in the central valley, and transformed the sleepy village of San Francisco into a teeming city.

Even the southern part of the state, remote as it was from the goldfields, was by no means unaffected. Indeed, it fully shared in the general prosperity of the new era. For cattle raising had long been the leading — and indeed almost the only — industry there, and from 1849 onward the ranchers had but to drive their herds northward to find a ready market for them, and at prices that a few years earlier would have been deemed fantastic.

135

But while gold mining continued to be an important factor in the economy of the state for several decades longer, the methods employed presently underwent radical changes, one of the results of which was that far fewer men were engaged in it. For by the mid-1850s virtually all the gold had been washed from the thousands of once-rich placer claims. Thereafter other techniques came into use; namely, quartz and hydraulic mining, both of which were complicated and expensive operations in which but few of the original gold hunters had any part.

Thus as the placer claims were one by one exhausted a wholesale exodus from the towns and camps of the Mother Lode got under way. Many of the Argonauts made their way back to their old homes on the east coast or elsewhere, a few in possession of sizable fortunes wrested from the Sierra creek-beds, the majority richer only in experience. But a goodly number of the ex-miners chose to remain and to cast their lots with the new state.

It was these, together with the few old-timers who had been living in California in pre-Gold Rush days, plus many later arrivals, who laid the foundations for the next great era in the annals of the state. This was the period, extending from the middle 1850s to well into the 1880s, when the agricultural resources of the region saw their first large-scale development. Scores of thousands of acres were put under cultivation from one end of the state to the other; orchards and vineyards were set out in the fertile coastal and interior valleys, and California's fruits and wines and cereals began to make their appearance in the markets of the world.

The most spectacular development of this period took place in the broad central valleys of the Sacramento and the San Joaquin. For there a series of immense ranches came into being, many covering areas of 30,000 acres or more. On most of these but a single crop was grown: wheat. It was specialized farming on a scale never before known in this country, with the employees on some ranches numbering into the hundreds during the planting and harvesting seasons. In the late 1890s these large-scale operations provided Frank Norris with the theme for his best-known novel, *The Octopus*.

Eventually two factors combined to bring the era of the wheat to a close: the exhaustion of the soil due to planting it to the same crop year after year, and the rise of the Argentine as a major wheat-producing nation. But during the industry's brief heyday, the owners lived like the landed barons of old, their ranch houses standing in the midst of veritable villages, with long rows of buildings serving as living quarters and mess halls for employees, huge barns for the hundreds of draft horses needed to plant and harvest the crop and haul it to the nearest railroad or river landing, sheds sheltering the plows, sowers, threshing machines, and other agricultural implements, and much else.

The pretentious houses of many of these early-day wheat kings have long since disappeared. A few, however, remain, scattered the length of the valley from the vicinity of Red Bluff to Fresno and beyond: begabled structures, usually two or three stories high, that stand, surrounded by clumps of venerable shade trees, and often with a cluster of ramshackle barns, stables, and other buildings nearby. These are truly relics of a bygone era, for in all but a few instances the great ranches of which they were the headquarters have long since been broken up. Today the former wheat fields are occupied by scores of moderate-sized farms, planted to orchards, vineyards, and a wide variety of other crops.

The period of the wheat, that is, the '60s, '70s, and '80s, of the last century, was a time of far-reaching changes elsewhere in California, the chief characteristics of which were accelerated industrial and commercial activity, the exploitation of the state's natural resources on a scale never before approached, and the rise of a numerous new group of financial titans. It was also an era of lamentably bad taste on the part not only of the new-rich enterprisers but of virtually all segments of the population, a circumstance that led later generations to bestow on it the ironical title of the Gilded Age.

Today the social, cultural, and artistic shortcomings of the Gilded Age have for the most part faded from the memories of even the oldest inhabitants and are recalled only in books or magazine articles treating reminiscently of the quaint manners and customs of our forebears. In one field, however, relics of that flamboyant era are very much with us: that is, in the field of architecture. It was, as still-existing examples of that period make clear, a time when the designers of the nation's buildings — and in particular the more ostentatious of its residences — threw all restraint to the winds and produced the extraordinary structures we now describe as belonging to the rococo, mid-Victorian, or carpenters' Gothic, school.

While the liking for such complex assemblages of towers, gables, dormers, and spires was by no means confined to any one locality, there is reason to believe that the movement reached its most luxuriant flowering in California. This was particularly true as it pertained to domestic architecture, the reason being that whereas in most other parts of the country the more elaborate private dwellings were often built of bricks or stone, on the west coast wood was all but universally used. Hence, to follow the prevailing mode was much easier — and less expensive — here than elsewhere, wood being a far more pliant substance than stone. The consequence was that throughout that period the California craftsmen industriously applied themselves to their lathes and jigsaws, turning out the prodigious quantities of "millwork" that embellished the façades of every residence with any claim to elegance.

While there was hardly a town throughout the length and breadth of the state that did not boast at least a few such ornate structures, it was in San Francisco that the movement reached its apex. Generally considered the city's most impressive example of mid-Victorian architecture — as it was certainly the most conspicuous — was the Hopkins mansion atop Nob Hill, a truly remarkable structure put up in the late 1870s, which remained visible from every part of the city until its destruction in the holocaust of April 18, 1906. It, however, was by no means alone, for scores of other big wooden residences, some only a shade less awesome in their outlines, lined San Francisco's streets, not only on the heights of Nob and Russian hills but on both sides of Van Ness Avenue and in the newly laid-out Western Addition, which lay just beyond.

Nor was this vogue for Victorian elegance confined to the homes of the wealthy. For throughout the final third of the century there were built literally thousands of modest dwellings in various parts of the city, all of which faithfully followed the prevailing mode. What is more, many of these, having escaped the 1906 fire, are still standing today: rows of two-story structures, all built to the same general plan. Crowded close together on twenty-foot lots, each has its bay window in front, together with a brave showing of "millwork" ornamenting virtually every square inch of its façade.

The interior arrangements of these houses are, like their baroque exteriors, all alike. The lower floor, reached by a short flight of steps from the sidewalk's edge, consists of entrance hall, on one side of which are stairs leading to the rooms above, while on the other is a series of three doors. The first of these opens into the front parlor, a chamber that in the old days was used only to entertain visitors on formal calls and at other times shunned by members of the household. Next came the back parlor, sometimes called the music room, a less formal sanctum where the family gathered evenings and which on gala occasions could be opened into the front parlor by sliding back the intervening doors, making them in effect a single room. Beyond was the dining room, and in the rear, its windows commanding a view of the tiny back yard, was the kitchen. In the basement, which commonly had a tradesmen's entrance opening on the street, were the wood and coal bins, storage space for foodstuffs and other household supplies, and, in one corner, a tiny cubicle, grandly termed the maid's room, where the kitchen slavey slept.

Upstairs were the front and back bedrooms, the first having a bay window identical with that of the front parlor beneath; this was the domain of the master and mistress of the house. The adjoining chamber was often used as a sewing room, while farther to the rear were one or two smaller rooms, the sleeping quarters of the children. Hence the houses, for all their narrow, cramped appearance when viewed from the street, had a degree of spaciousness, for each contained· a minimum of eight rooms and frequently as many as ten — ample to shelter in reasonable comfort the by no means small families of the period.

One of California's best-known residences and among the most impressive existing examples of the highly ornate style of architecture in vogue during the latter half of the last century, is the Carson House at Eureka. Built in the mid-1880s, it has long been a major attraction of that north-coast lumbering town, both to residents and visitors, and there is rarely a time during the daylight hours when groups are not to be seen gathered before its prim iron fence gazing in awe at the assemblage of towers, turrets, porticoes, and gables that comprise its exterior.

The man responsible for the building of this extraordinarily complex structure, and who lived in it for many years, was William Carson, pioneer Humboldt County lumberman, who had arrived at Eureka in the early days, established one of the first sawmills in the redwood forests of the region, and, having prospered, set about in the early 1880s laying plans for the construction of a residence in keeping with his new estate. The site chosen was on the crest of a little hill, from which the owner could look down on his big mills and lumberyards on the bay shore and on the ships arriving in the harbor to carry his products off to the markets of the world.

It is said that Carson gave his architect carte blanche in the design and construction of his new home, insisting only that the materials and workmanship be of the best obtainable. Clearly the other took him at

140

56. Carson House, Eureka. Of California's many surviving
examples of Victorian architecture, this is generally acknowl-
edged to be the most striking. Built by an early-day lumber
magnate (whose big sawmills were close by), it stands at the
corner of Second and M streets, its complicated roof-line and
extraordinarily ornate tower visible from all parts of the city.
Admirably preserved, it now houses one of Eureka's service
clubs. *Photograph from the Eureka Chamber of Commerce, Eureka*

his word, for into its construction went mahoganies from Central and South America, teak from the Orient, oak and other hardwoods, plus the finest grades of seasoned redwood from Carson's own mills. Moreover, the craftsmanship throughout was such as to win the admiration of present-day artisans, every detail of its finish, from the paneling and moldings of its big downstairs rooms to the extraordinarily lavish decorations of the exterior, being executed with a skill and meticulous precision rarely seen in this hurried modern age.

Because of these circumstances the house was, understandably, a long time building and it was not until 1886 that the proud owner moved in. "Bill" Carson lived there for the remainder of his life, and it is said that during his last years it was his custom to climb daily to the tower atop the structure and from its windows scan the horizon to the west, watching for the appearance of the little lumber schooners in which the bulk of his lumber was shipped. Following his death, the house was occupied by Milton Carson, elder son of its builder, and when he, too, died, it was presently taken over by a local civic organization, the Ingomar Club, by which it and its grounds have since been carefully maintained as one of the most interesting and historically valuable relics of the city's past.

In recent years Hollywood has been by no means unaware of the structure's unique pictorial qualities, and the old mansion has frequently appeared in films as an authentic background for dramas laid in the 1880s or earlier. Tourists, too, rarely fail to seek out the house, which stands at the corner of Second and M streets, and there is considerable justification for the claim often made that it is "the most photographed home in all the west."

At the corner of 16th and H streets in Sacramento stands a big wooden structure that for more than half a century has been the official residence of California's governors. Built in the mid-1870s, the old mansion, three stories high, its exterior a complex mass of bay windows,

57. Governor's Mansion, Sacramento. This ornate Victorian dwelling at the corner of Sixteenth and H streets was built in the mid-1870s by a pioneer merchant named Albert Gallatin. In 1903 it was acquired by the state as the governor's residence and has ever since served that purpose.
Photograph by the Sacramento Bee, *Sacramento*

towers, turrets, and gables, all heavily ornamented with the scrolls and curlicues once known as "millwork," is, like Eureka's Carson House, a prize example of the type of home put up by prosperous citizens all over the nation two or three generations ago.

But while the Governor's Mansion is definitely a period piece, the product of an age when, by modern standards, domestic architecture was deplorably overornate, yet the building has a dignity and imposing quality that impresses even casual observers. Standing in the midst of grounds that cover half a city block, and surrounded by an elaborate iron fence, with a granite-paved driveway leading to the porte-cochere, and thence to a charmingly baroque little carriage house in the rear, it perfectly symbolizes an age and a way of life that have long since disappeared.

The house, designed by an architect named Nathaniel D. Goodell, was built in 1877 for Albert Gallatin, one of the leading citizens of the town, who was long manager of the firm of Huntington & Hopkins, dealers in hardware, building supplies, mining and farming machinery since gold rush days. In 1888 the property was sold to another prominent local merchant, Joseph Steffens, partner in a prosperous paint firm. Steffens is remembered today mainly for the stable of race horses he maintained and for the fact that he was the father of Lincoln Steffens, widely known editor and member of the "muckraker" group of journalists who were much in the public eye during the early years of the present century.

In 1903 the property was purchased by the state as the governor's residence and has ever since served that purpose. Meantime the city's business section has steadily spread out in that direction so that today the old mansion is virtually surrounded by stores, service stations, and other commercial establishments. Consequently, in recent years proposals have frequently been made for the building of a more modern governor's residence. These proposals have, however, been opposed by recent holders of that office, including Earl Warren and Goodwin

58. Stanford Home, Sacramento. Long one of the showplaces of the early town, the thirty-eight-room Stanford
Mansion stands at the corner of Eighth and N streets. Here
was born Leland Stanford, Jr., and it was upon his death at
the age of fifteen that his parents founded the great university at Palo Alto that bears his name.   *Photograph by the*
McCurry Studio, *Sacramento*

Knight, who have maintained that the historic building is not only quite comfortable but so soundly constructed that it is capable of continuing to serve its purpose for many years to come.

In support of that view, a Sacramento newspaper recently pronounced it "one of those good, old-fashioned, roomy houses with spacious apartments, high ceilings, hardwood floors and . . . wide closets," that possess a charm and livability frequently lacking in many modern residences. Its bay windows, mansard roof, and highly ornamental tower enclose three stories of spacious rooms. The main entrance opens into a wide hall; to the right are the library and study and, on the left, are two reception rooms, each 18 by 30 feet, which can be thrown together on gala occasions. The two upper floors contain eight bedrooms, plus ample storage space. All the main rooms have handsome marble fireplaces, and the entire property is kept in excellent repair, making it an extremely interesting and historically significant example of a type of domestic architecture that has now all but vanished from view.

Another of Sacramento's many ornate residences dating from the 1860s or earlier is the Stanford House, now known as the Stanford-Lathrop Memorial Home, which stands at the southeast corner of Eighth and N streets, two blocks to the west of Capitol Park, in what was long the most exclusive residential district of the city. In 1900 the property, which then had been vacant since the Stanfords moved to San Francisco some twenty-five years earlier, was presented to the Roman Catholic Diocese of Sacramento by Stanford's widow, together with an endowment of $75,000, and it has ever since been used for charitable purposes, mainly as an orphanage for children of all ages. During all that time it has been carefully maintained, with some of the downstairs rooms restored and furnished much as they were when the Stanfords occupied them. It is open to the public daily from 2 to 5 P.M., and thousands visit it each year.

146

59. Parlor of the Stanford Home. Carefully preserved and open to the public, these downstairs rooms are much as they were when the Stanfords lived there during the 1860s and 1870s. On the wall above the piano are portraits of Governor Stanford and his wife. *Photograph by the* Sacramento Bee, *Sacramento*

60. E. B. Crocker House, Sacramento. One of the most pretentious of Sacramento's early residences, this structure, dating from the 1860s, was built for a pioneer banker, B. F. Hastings. Later it was bought by Judge Crocker, who built next door the gallery — shown at the left — to house his collection of European art. Both the dwelling and the adjoining structure are now known as the E. B. Crocker Art Gallery. *Photograph by McCurry Studio, Sacramento*

PART IV: THE AGE OF THE MOGULS

The house was originally built by a prosperous Sacramento merchant named Sheldon C. Fogus. It was then a two-story brick structure, "furnished in a costly manner inside and out," according to a contemporary account, with a single-story wing on one side. The whole was set on a spacious lot occupying a quarter of the block, on which stood, too, a brick stable, fruit trees, and ornamental shrubbery, and enclosed by a high picket fence.

Stanford purchased the property in the summer of 1861, at a time when he was a nominee for governor of California, to which office he was elected on September 4 of that year. The governor's early months in his new residence were full of incident. For the winter of 1861-62 was an exceptionally rainy one, with a succession of storms farther up the valley raising the river to a point where it overflowed its banks and flooded much of the city. Thus on the morning Stanford took office, January 10, 1862, the water was so high that when he left his house for the inaugural ceremonies he had to travel by rowboat, and when he returned a few hours later he gained entrance through a second-floor window.

As soon as the waters subsided, however, not only was the flood damage repaired but an extensive program of improvements got under way. These last included the building of a second wing, measuring 32 by 18 feet, designed to serve as the governor's office. The ground floor of the main building, measuring 46 by 40 feet, was given over to two spacious salons, one on each side of the central hallway. The ceilings of these chambers were 16 feet high and their walls and doorways were richly decorated with panels and architraves of carved oak. Although Stanford had paid but $8,000 for the property, these additions and refurbishings are said to have cost several times that amount. Ten years later, in 1872, other extensive improvements were undertaken. These involved raising the main house and building an additional story beneath, thereby giving the structure the appearance it has today.

During the interval between these first and second rebuildings, the owner had amassed great wealth through his participation in the building and operation of the western half of the first transcontinental railroad. Consequently, in the 1872 rehabilitation, cost was a lightly regarded detail. Soon after its reopening in February of the following year a description of its wonders appeared in a San Francisco newspaper, from which we learn that "everything is on a scale of unsurpassed magnificence." Among the attractions listed were "lace curtains of the finest fabrics" and, adorning the walls and ceilings of the downstairs rooms, "frescoes beautiful in design and exquisite in artistic perfection."

Here many brilliant social affairs took place during Stanford's term as governor and later. It was here, too, that the couple's only child, Leland, Jr., was born, and it was the youth's death, at the age of fifteen, that led to the founding by his parents of the Stanford University of Palo Alto. The Stanfords took great pride in their son and throughout his brief life were at pains to see that he got every advantage their wealth and position could bestow.

The story is told that a few weeks after Leland, Jr's, birth, a large dinner was given to celebrate the event, at the close of which an immense silver platter was brought in and deposited in the center of the table. When its cover was removed, the hosts' son and heir was revealed beneath, lying on a bed of spring blossoms. The infant was then carried about the table to be admired by each guest. By all accounts he stood the ordeal well, for he was said to have been smiling and gurgling all the while.

Two details of the house that rarely fail to interest visitors are objects reflecting its owner's connection with the first overland railroad. On a chandelier in the dining room are still to be seen two glass shades, on the sides of which are etched the likeness of a pioneer locomotive Also, Stanford's bookcase has at its top a carved replica of an early engine and passenger car, together with the ornate letter "S" on each of its frosted glass doors.

PART IV: THE AGE OF THE MOGULS

Close to the river, at the corner of Second and O streets, in a district long since given over to small shops and rooming houses, a majority of them far advanced toward decay, stands an impressive relic of the period when many of Sacramento's wealthy and socially prominent families made their homes there. This now houses the Crocker Art Gallery, long one of the city's major cultural institutions.

Built in the early 1860s by a pioneer banker and later bought by Judge E. B. Crocker, a leading attorney and brother of Charles Crocker, co-owner of the western half of the pioneer Central Pacific Railroad, the big mansion, its exterior replete with the bay windows and scroll-work characteristic of mid-Victorian architecture, is now owned by the city and, together with its two-story annex, contains an extensive collection of paintings, drawings, and sculptures assembled by its first owner.

Soon after his house was completed, Judge Crocker and his wife toured Europe, and it was in Paris — then just recovering from the disastrous Franco-Prussian War — that he acquired — at, it was said, bargain prices — the nucleus of his art collection. On later visits these were added to and, in order properly to display his purchases, he presently built on the grounds adjacent to his residence a handsome art gallery. While a good part of the hundreds of paintings and drawings he assembled were by artists no longer regarded as belonging to the first rank, the collection nonetheless has its quota of authentic masterpieces. Among the latter are drawings by Watteau and Holbein, studies by Michelangelo, Rembrandt, and Leonardo Da Vinci, together with Van Dyck's "Christ Healing the Blind," Dürer's "Saint Joseph and the Virgin Mary," Guido Reni's "The Entombment of Christ," Murrillo's "Gypsy," a portrait by Rubens, and a number of others.

Following Crocker's death, his widow, in 1884, presented the collection, together with the building in which it was housed, to the city of Sacramento. Later the residence next door was also acquired, whereupon the two buildings were joined and the whole has since been maintained as the E. B. Crocker Art Gallery. It is open daily to the public.

Visitors to the premises today find the rooms of the old house itself no less interesting than the paintings hanging on its walls. For the spacious ground floor chambers with their tall, narrow windows, high ceilings, and the intricately wrought woodwork of their doorways and floors, bear impressive testimony to the grandeur and elegance of the wealthy of a bygone generation.

Yet another of Sacramento's impressive Victorian residences is the Heilbron Mansion which stands at the corner of Seventh and O streets, a begabled, three-story building surrounded by an iron fence and shaded by century-old black walnut trees. Built in the early 1880s, the house was long the home of August Heilbron, pioneer cattleman and hardware merchant, whose descendants continued to live there until the mid-1950s when it became a tearoom and restaurant.

In converting the old building to commercial uses, the new tenants wisely chose to preserve, inside and out, the appearance and atmosphere of an earlier age. Virtually the only concessions to modernity were the substitution of electricity for gas in the elaborate brass-and-crystal chandeliers, of central heating to supplement that furnished by the numerous fireplaces, and the installation of an air-conditioning system. The consequence is that visitors to its spacious, ornate rooms can easily imagine themselves transported backward to the sort of environment in which prosperous citizens lived three-quarters of a century ago.

The exterior conforms closely to the more pretentious type of residence put up in many parts of the nation in the 1870s and 1880s, with a high basement elevating the main floor some eight feet above the street level, and with bay windows projecting outward on both sides of the main entrance and terminating in dormers at their crests.

Within, the series of big, lofty chambers well reflect the domestic setting preferred in the days of one's grandparents. Of particular interest are the hand-painted ceilings of the dining room and front and back parlors, their once-bright colors now subdued and mellowed. Well

61. Hallway of the Crocker House. In 1884, following the death of Judge Crocker, his widow presented his gallery and collection of European art to the city of Sacramento. Later the city also acquired the Crocker home and the two structures were joined, becoming the E. B. Crocker Art Gallery.
Photograph by Wyland Stanley, San Francisco

62.· Octagonal House, San Francisco. During the middle
and late 1850s there was a vogue for eight-sided residences in
various parts of the United States, the chief advantage claimed
for·them being that by this arrangement each room received a
maximum of sunshine at all seasons of the year. Eight such
houses were built in San Francisco, of which two still stand,
one on Russian Hill and the other — pictured above — on
Gough Street near the corner of Union.   *Photograph by Fred
Lyon, Sausalito*

worthy of notice, too, is the intricately wrought woodwork throughout and the graceful Italian marble fireplaces to be seen not only in the main ground-floor chambers but in the numerous bed- and sitting rooms above.

Of the many types of residences built in San Francisco during the early days, perhaps the most curious were the octagon houses, of which two are still standing. These strange, eight-sided structures were once to been seen in other parts of the nation, all built during the decade from 1855 to 1865. It has been estimated that their total numbered between fifty and sixty, of which two were on Long Island, two in Michigan, one each in Wisconsin and Mississippi, and the balance at various other places. They were, however, more numerous in San Francisco than in any other city, a total of eight having been erected there in the middle and late 1850s. Of these, four stood on Russian Hill.

The fad for eight-sided dwellings is said to have been the result of the appearance in 1853 of a book entitled *A Home for All; or, the Granite Wall and Octagon Mode of Building*, by Orson Squire Fowler, published by R. Walls of New York. Among other advantages claimed for them was that their octagon shape offered less resistance to the wind and thus rendered them safer in regions where tornadoes were frequent; also that the placing of windows on all eight sides assured a maximum of light and sunshine in every room at all seasons of the year.

It was probably the second of these purported superiorities over the usual mode of construction that appealed to early San Franciscans. For, then as now, the city was often shrouded in fogs sweeping in from the ocean, a circumstance that made sunshine doubly welcome. How well these theories worked out in practice must be left to conjecture, for, so far as is known, none of the pioneer owners has left behind any record of his findings on these points. Occupants of the two structures still standing have, however, stated that this type of construction has certain disadvantages, the chief of which is that their unconventional shape results in serious inconveniences in the arrangement of their interiors. An elderly spinster lady who had long lived in one of the houses recently stated upon moving out that the placing of furniture in the odd-shaped rooms had presented a problem, and besides it had been "hard to keep clean."

The two octagon houses that still remain in San Francisco are much alike in appearance, both being of about the same size, two stories in height, and with four rooms on each floor. However, the materials used in their construction differ widely. One, located at 1051 Green Street, atop Russian Hill, has thick outer walls of a concretelike substance, the latter composed, it is said, of "burned lime mixed with alluvial clay." That this mixture resulted in an eminently sturdy material is indicated by the fact that the structure remains in prime condition today, having withstood the wear and tear of almost a full century and passed undamaged through the violent earthquake of 1906. The second, some six blocks to the west, on Gough Street near the corner of Union, is of all-wood construction, and it, too, has borne its ninety years with grace.

Both houses have been continuously occupied since they were first put up. That on Green Street, now surrounded by more pretentious residences and multiple-story apartment houses, remains a private dwelling, its venerable stone walls covered with ivy and all but hidden from the street by the trees and shrubs of its old-fashioned garden. The Gough Street house, known to generations of children living in the neighborhood as "the Inkwell" — a not inappropriate name considering its shape and the small eight-sided cupola at the apex of its roof — has recently been converted to other uses. For in 1952 it was moved across the street from its original location and taken over by the National Society of Colonial Dames to serve as the western headquarters of that organization.

In the early days several other of these quaint structures were put up in the area adjacent to San Francisco. Of these, two are still stand-

63. Early Octagonal House, San Francisco. This view from Rincon Hill, taken in the 1860s, shows one of a number of eight-sided houses then standing in the town. It has long since disappeared. *Photograph by Wyland Stanley, San Francisco*

64. Stanford Mansion, San Francisco. Upon moving to San Francisco following the completion of the Central Pacific Railroad in 1869, Stanford built this impressive residence atop Nob Hill. To the left is seen a portion of the turreted home of his railroad partner, Mark Hopkins; both were destroyed in the fire of 1906. *Photograph from the Sutter's Fort Museum, Sacramento*

ing. One, located on the peninsula to the south of the city, is a small wooden building that long served as a carriage house on the country estate of a pioneer resident. The other, a far more impressive edifice, is located in the rolling foothills of Sonoma County, about four miles to the northwest of the town of Petaluma and some forty miles north of San Francisco. The latter was built in the early 1860s by one Silas Martin, owner of much land in the district, who by family tradition followed two trades: those of nurseryman and harness maker.

The house, standing on a knoll overlooking a pleasant rural valley, today is surrounded by a grove of lofty redwoods and wide-spreading walnut trees. It is said that the redwoods, of which there were originally six — five still survive — were set out at intervals to commemorate the births of Martin's six sons. The old building itself, with its concrete walls and meticulously fashioned doorways, windows, and inner partitions shows but few evidences of its more than ninety years, and this despite the fact that during one twenty-year period it stood vacant.

One striking architectural feature of the original structure has, however, long since disappeared: the wide porch that formerly extended entirely around it, and onto which doorways opened out from both the first and second floors. That the builders of the old house were highly skilled is evident from the spiral stairway that rises to the second story from a little circular hallway in the center of the structure, an uncommonly graceful example of the craftsmanship of early-day stair-makers. Another notable feature of the property is that the venerable house still remains in possession of descendants of its original owner, no less than five generations of Martins having lived there.

Long the domain of San Francisco's plutocrats was the crest of Nob Hill which, rising in a series of steep inclines from the business district on the flats below, dominates the entire central part of the city. In the late 1860s and early 1870s, a group of wealthy citizens, finding warehouses, factories, and other commercial establishments encroaching on their former homes on Rincon Hill and South Park, began moving to its lofty crest, where they put up a cluster of mansions that in size and pretentiousness excelled anything then known on the entire west coast.

One of the most eye-filling of these was the baroque Crocker residence, home of Charles Crocker of the railroad Big Four, which stood at the northwest corner of California and Taylor streets, on the present site of the Grace Cathedral. Opposite it, on the block bounded by California, Taylor, and Sacramento streets, was an austere white mansion, said to have been a replica of an Italian palace, owned successively by two other early railroad magnates, David D. Colton and Collis P. Huntington. The lot on which it stood was later presented to the city by Huntington's widow and is a public park, much frequented by nursemaids and their young charges from the towering hotels and apartments that now crown the hill.

A block farther to the south, where the California Street hill tilts downward toward the business districts, were the adobes of Mark Hopkins and Leland Stanford, the last-named a three-story Victorian pile in the best manner of the period, and the other a weird aggregation of towers and cupolas which its owner — who did not live long enough to occupy it — dubbed the "Hotel de Hopkins." Because the horse-drawn vehicles of the day had difficulty scaling the steep, cobble-paved streets from below, Stanford financed the building of the California Street Cable Railroad, the tiny cars of which daily brought loads of admiring visitors past his door.

All these big structures, together with scores of others hardly less impressive, were swept away in the fire that followed the jolting earthquake on the morning of April 18, 1906. Today the sole survivor of the group is the big brownstone mansion that occupies the northwest corner of California and Mason streets, built by ex-saloon-keeper James L. Flood with profits reaped from the fabulously rich Nevada silver

65. Interior, Flood Mansion, San Francisco. Flood's big brownstone house atop Nob Hill was the only residence in that area to escape the holocaust of April 18, 1906. For although its interior was consumed by the flames, its walls remained intact. The structure was later rebuilt and today houses the Pacific Union Club. *Photograph by Wyland Stanley, San Francisco*

66. Whittier House, San Francisco. Standing at the corner of Jackson and Laguna streets, this 30-room sandstone residence was put up in the 1890s by William Frank Whittier, pioneer merchant. Today it serves as headquarters of the long-established California Historical Society. *Photograph from the California Historical Society, San Francisco*

mines, and now housing the Pacific Union Club. The Flood house, too, fell victim to the all-devouring flames, but unlike its neighbors, its outer walls were of stone and thus withstood the fire virtually undamaged. The property was later acquired by the club, its interior rebuilt and two semicircular wings added to its north and south sides.

The original house, long celebrated as the only brownstone residence west of the Rockies, is said to have cost its owner well over a million dollars. One of its outstanding features was — and is — the handsome stone and bronze fence that surrounds the property. Tradition states that all during the years when Flood lived there one servant was permanently assigned to the task of keeping its metal parts polished to a dazzling brightness.

Another picturesque survivor of the San Francisco mansions of the 1890s and earlier is the thirty-room red sandstone Whittier house which stands at the southeast corner of Jackson and Laguna streets, occupying a hilltop site that commands a sweeping view of the bay and the Golden Gate. Put up in the mid-1890s by William Frank Whittier, pioneer merchant and capitalist, it was long one of the city's showplaces, the scene of many brilliant social functions during the gaslight era. The house was well laid out to accommodate such gatherings, its ground floor boasting not only uncommonly spacious living and dining rooms but a ballroom measuring 36 by 54 feet.

The finish throughout is in the best style of the period, the entrance hall, 24 by 32 feet, being paneled in carved oak, the living room and its adjoining Oriental smoking room in mahogany, and the dining room in imported tamanu wood. The fireplaces in all the main chambers are of Italian marble, elaborately carved, that in the living room being particularly impressive for its intricately fashioned overmantel. The numerous bedrooms and sitting rooms that occupy the upper two floors are no less elegant in their appointments, the stairways, doors, and other fittings being of rare woods and the hardware of hand-wrought German silver.

During the sixty years of its existence the old house has had a singularly checkered history. Having survived the earthquake and fire of 1906, it remained in possession of descendants of its original owner until 1941, when it was sold to the German government and became the consulate of that Nazi-dominated land. During the brief interval until the United States entered World War II it was the scene of elaborate functions given by the local consul, Fritz Wiedermann, congenital party-giver and close friend of Adolph Hilter. With the outbreak of hostilities Wiedermann fled the country and for the next several years the house and its contents were under the jurisdiction of the Alien Property Custodian.

After the war it reverted to private ownership, passing through several hands until, in the spring of 1956, it was purchased by the California Historical Society for use as a permanent headquarters of that long-established organization. In refitting the premises for this new use every care was taken to make no changes that would alter the appearance of the old structure as it was in its heyday. Thus in future years visitors to the spot will have an opportunity to view the elaborate domestic setting in which prosperous citizens lived in the horse-and-buggy days before the turn of the century.

Toward the middle of the last century a new type of architecture, known as the "Gothic Revival," began to make its appearance, first in England and on the continent, then in the United States. This style, embodying the pointed arch on towers, gables, windows, and other features, was widely adopted by the architects of the day, not only in churches and other public buildings but, to an extent, in private dwellings. The movement spread to California in the years following the gold rush, the most conspicuous examples being Old St. Mary's Church in San Francisco, begun in 1853, together with St. Anne's at Columbia, and St. James' at Sonora, built, respectively, in 1856 and 1859.

The Gothic motif was evident, too, in a number of residences put up in California towns during the 1850s and 1860s, but most of these have long since disappeared, victims either of the frequent early-day fires or torn down to make way for more modern structures. Of the few examples that still survive, one of the most interesting is the Moss Cottage in Oakland, which today stands in Mosswood Park, a spacious city playground and recreation center at the corner of Broadway and 38th Street. Built in 1865 for J. Mora Moss, a prominent merchant, it has long been regarded by authorities as a near-perfect example of the application of Gothic decorative principles to domestic architecture.

The cottage is two stories in height, the most notable feature of its façade being three pointed gables projecting from its second floor, the largest extending out over the main entrance and the others above the windows of the parlor on one side and of the library on the other. Within, the principal rooms open off a broad central hall, from which a graceful stairway, "guarded with a Gothic open balustrade," leads to the chambers above. All the downstairs rooms, and in particular the parlor and library, are elegantly finished, the Gothic motif being carried out not only in the design of the fireplaces and the panels of the doors but in the intricately carved moldings on walls and ceilings, and even in the design of the plaster cartouches from which hang the elaborate gas fixtures.

Throughout the structure every detail of the workmanship has a finish and precision that reflect high credit on the craftsmen who had a hand in its building.

The discovery, in 1859, of rich deposits of silver on the slopes of Nevada's Sun Mountain marked the beginning of a new and grandiose era in San Francisco. During the next decade and a half new wealth flowed into the city in a mighty stream, energizing all phases of its business life and transforming a group of former merchants, innkeepers, bankers, and speculators into multimillionaires.

One of their number was William Chapman Ralston, picturesque financial plunger whose Bank of California, through its branch in

67. Ralston House, Belmont. Originally a small villa put up in 1854 by an Italian political refugee named Count Cipriani, the property was purchased a decade later by the San Francisco banker, William C. Ralston, who proceeded to transform it into one of the largest and most luxurious of the peninsula country estates. Today it is one of the buildings of a Catholic school, its former ballroom converted into a chapel. *Photograph by Wyland Stanley, San Francisco*

Virginia City, enabled him and his partners to gain control of several of the Comstock Lode's most profitable mines. With the funds flowing in from that source, Ralston launched a series of spectacular enterprises: the building of the Palace Hotel, the establishment of steamship lines, water companies, a theater, and so many other projects that he presently became known as "the man who built San Francisco."

Not the least impressive of Ralston's accomplishments was the building of Belmont, his huge, rambling residence down the peninsula, where for a decade and longer he entertained on a scale previously unknown on the west coast. When he acquired the property, which was situated on a pleasantly wooded hillside some twenty miles south of San Francisco, it was occupied only by a modest little villa. However, he at once began an extensive building program, adding story after story and wing after wing to the original structure, laying out elaborate gardens, and constructing greenhouses, stables, and quarters for the small army of household servants, gardeners, grooms, and other retainers needed to maintain the establishment.

Everything was done on a scale that set new standards even in that age of ostentation. The stables housing his scores of horses were fitted up with a degree of elegance rarely seen even in the more pretentious homes of the period, the stalls being finished in mahogany inlaid with mother-of-pearl, and in the harness room the gleaming harnesses and other equipment were hung from hooks of solid silver. One of the many outlying buildings was a gymnasium, containing a fully equipped Turkish bath, with trained attendants constantly on duty. For the proper illumination of the property Ralston built a gasworks, and to assure an adequate supply of water, installed a dam and reservoir higher in the hills, plus an elaborate distribution system.

It was, however, on the house itself that the greatest care was expended. Because Ralston was a man of markedly convivial instincts, and because he had constituted himself the unofficial host to distinguished visitors passing through San Francisco, groups of guests were constantly enjoying his hospitality, their number rarely less than twenty and frequently reaching several times that many. For their proper accommodation he several times enlarged the mansion; one authority states that by 1868 the big, rambling building could comfortably put up as many as 120.

Throughout his career Ralston had a flair for the dramatic and nothing pleased him more than to astound his guests at Belmont by some spectacular surprise. Sometimes this took the form of the viands set before them in the big dining room, as on the occasion when the main course of the three-hour-long repast consisted of "a humming-bird filled with baked almonds, surrounded by a Spring linnet, which, in turn, was enveloped by an English snipe." Another of his favorite devices was to assemble his guests in the library, the chairs and divans of which had all been arranged to face in the same direction; then, after a period of waiting, the entire wall before them rose slowly upward and disappeared into the ceiling, revealing the well-laden, snowy-white tables of the banquet hall, an army of Chinese waiters standing at attention.

The spectacular failure of Ralston's bank in the summer of 1875, and his subsequent drowning in the waters of the bay, brought Belmont's opulent period to a sudden close. The property passed into the hands of William Sharon, banker and ex-senator from Nevada. Later it was taken over as a private hospital for mental patients and, finally, as a Catholic school, which it remains today. While much of its former splendor has long since disappeared, those who nowadays visit the spot may see relics of the period when Belmont was celebrated all over the West for the unprecedented lavishness of the hospitality dispensed there.

Some half dozen miles farther down the peninsula from Ralston's Belmont there stood until recently a handsome frame dwelling representative of the residences put up by prosperous Californians during the 1860s, a period just before the beginning of mid-Victorian flamboyance in domestic architecture that was to reach full flower during the next

68. Interior, Ralston's Belmont. In the years prior to the failure of his bank in 1875 and his subsequent suicide in the waters of the bay, Ralston was generally acclaimed San Francisco's first citizen, and few were the visitors of note who passed through the city without becoming guests at Belmont.
Photograph by Wyland Stanley, San Francisco

69. Valparaiso Park, Atherton. One of the first families to settle down the peninsula to the south of San Francisco was that of Faxon Dean Atherton who in 1860 acquired a mile-square of oak-studded meadowlands there and built the austere but comfortable house pictured above. Valparaiso Park, as the estate was called, was for a time the home of the well-known novelist, Gertrude Atherton, who had married one of the sons of the family. *Photograph from the California State Library, Sacramento*

two decades. This austere, well-proportioned house was long the home of Faxon Dean Atherton, a native of Dedham, Massachusetts, who had begun his successful merchandising career in Chile where he had amassed a fortune, married a daughter of that country, and in 1859 had continued on to California. There he bought an extensive tract of land in the oak-strewn district now known as Atherton, christened it Valparaiso Park, and the next year built his commodious house.

Fortunately, a record of the sort of life lived at Valparaiso Park during the next several decades has been preserved for readers of the present day, for one of the sons of the family presently married a San Francisco belle named Gertrude Horn and took her to live on the family estate. Years later, she, who had meantime become the renowned writer, Gertrude Atherton, recalled much that had transpired there. Her recollections of the sedate life lived by the first families of the peninsula three quarters of a century ago, as set forth in her autobiography, *Adventures of a Novelist*, reveal that little of it was to her taste. By her account, the ladies of the household spent their mornings reading, writing letters, or strolling in the garden, and their afternoons sitting on the veranda, busily engaged in sewing, doing "fancy work," and chatting on subjects of an elevating nature. "I often wondered," wrote the energetic daughter-in-law of the family, "if life anywhere else in the whole world were so dull."

The house itself Gertrude Atherton describes as a large, comfortable structure, boasting two bathrooms — whereas most neighboring mansions had but one — comfortably furnished, and surrounded by extensive gardens featuring lawns, fountains, and an extraordinary variety of flowers and shrubs, both those native to the country and exotic plants imported from South America, the Orient, and elsewhere.

The head of the family had the true instincts of the patriarch, and as his numerous brood of sons and daughters grew up and married, it was his intention to build for each a house under the oaks of his mile-square estate. However, at the time Gertrude Atherton became a member of the clan only two of these subordinate structures had arisen: those of a daughter Alejandra, who had married a New Yorker, Major Lawrence Rathbone, and Gertrude's husband, George. Faxon Dean Atherton was not only an able businessman but also a man of scholarly interests, and for years he conducted a wide correspondence with Daniel Webster, Louis Agassiz, and other eminent figures in political and scientific circles, many of whom became guests at Valparaiso Park on their visits to the coast.

The first San Franciscans to settle "down the peninsula" were, like the Athertons, conservative by nature, people who lived sedate, well-ordered lives and sedulously avoided ostentation in any form. There was, accordingly, much dismay when it was learned that certain new-rich outsiders had purchased property in the area and planned to erect pretentious mansions there.

One of the first of these intruders was William C. Ralston, whose flamboyant estate at Belmont has been described. Another was James L. Flood, once owner of the Auction Lunch, a restaurant and bar that had long been a favorite gathering place for pioneer San Franciscans. With the discovery of silver ores in Nevada, Flood had, like virtually every other solvent citizen of the town, begun speculating in the stocks of the Comstock mines. More fortunate than most, he presently became part owner of the Con-Virginia, by far the richest of the properties on the Lode, which within a few years had made him many times a millionaire.

Having built his impressive brownstone town house on Nob Hill, he in 1878 began construction of Linden Towers, an extraordinary assemblage of turrets, towers, and gables that for the next six decades surpassed in magnificence the by no means modest country homes of his neighbors and became known from one end of California to the other as "Flood's Wedding Cake." Located at Menlo Park, some thirty miles south of San Francisco, Linden Towers well typified mid-Victorian ele-

70. Flood's Linden Towers, Menlo Park. When, in the late
1870s, a group of new-rich San Franciscans began building
elaborate mansions on the peninsula to the south of the city,
old-time residents were scornful of this invasion of their quiet
community. Thus when ex-barkeep James L. Flood put up
this ornate dwelling in 1878, the neighbors promptly dubbed
it "Flood's Wedding Cake." *Photograph from the California*
State Library, Sacramento

71. Library, Linden Towers. The interior of James L. Flood's peninsula home was fitted up on a scale no less magnificent than its exterior, as evidenced by this view of the library and, through the doorway to the left, a portion of an adjoining sitting room. *Photograph by Wyland Stanley, San Francisco*

72. Flood's Carriage House. Not only were the country residences of California's financial tycoons of the 1870s and later
highly complex in their architecture, but the lesser buildings
on their estates usually followd the same pattern. Above is a
view of the carriage house of James L. Flood's Linden Towers.
Photograph by Wyland Stanley, San Francisco

gance at its most luxuriant flowering. Not only was the house itself, with its lofty central tower and wide verandas (painted a dazzling white and thus visible for miles about), a triumph of the scrollworker's art, but its furnishings were fully in keeping with the tastes of the period, room after room being filled with carpets, cabinets, tapestries, and other objets d'art assembled from dealers both in this country and abroad.

The extensive grounds were laid out on a scale no less magnificent, the entire estate being enclosed in a high brick wall and the area about the mansion having acres of lawns and gardens, with scores of fountains and statues lining its walks and driveways. The Flood horses and carriages were housed in a handsome frame building far larger and more elegantly finished than most residences of the period, the stalls being of polished mahogany and the harness-room and grooms' quarters having not only walls of rare woods, but doorknobs and other fittings of sterling silver. Even the gate lodge, standing beside the main entrance to the estate, was an impressive little structure, finished inside and out in the opulent style of the whole, and giving arriving guests an advance hint of the magnificence soon to be revealed to them.

California has had its full share of what are loosely termed "freak houses"; that is, those which in design, arrangement, or other respects fail by a wide measure to conform to accepted principles of domestic architecture. Included in this category are the octagonal houses, previously described, that enjoyed a brief season of popularity, together with a variety of others dating from earliest times down to the present, in which owners or builders gave free rein to their highly unorthodox views on such matters.

Of the goodly number of houses of that sort to be found in California, one of the most curious is the big, sprawling Winchester Mansion, which stands in the upper end of the Santa Clara Valley, some five miles to the southwest of San Jose. The history of the structure is no less strange than its appearance. Sometime in the 1880s the property was bought by Mrs. Sarah L. Winchester, widow of a son of the founder of the Win-

73. Gate-House of Flood Estate. Typical of the architecture
of the period was this ornate little cottage that stood beside
the main entrance to James L. Flood's Linden Towers.
Photograph from the California State Library, Sacramento

74. The Winchester Mystery House near San José. View of part of the fantastic Winchester residence, which was thirty-eight years building, its owner having been told by a spiritualist that she would live as long as construction continued.
Photograph from the California Historical Society, San Franciso

chester Arms Company. At the time of her purchase, a spacious, seventeen-room residence was being erected there, and the new owner —whose husband and two children had recently died—was informed by a spiritualist whom she had consulted that she herself would live only so long as the building of the house continued.

The result was that when she took possession, the crews of carpenters and other artisans who had been working on the structure were all retained, and when the original building was finished, they set about putting up, first one addition, and then others. Thus was launched a program of building that was to last without interruption for well over a third of a century, and which terminated only with Mrs. Winchester's death in 1922. The house that resulted was, as might be expected, one of the most extraordinary ever built. Not only were new wings and extensions and appendages constantly being added until the structure eventually covered an area several acres in extent, but at the same time other workmen were kept busy making alterations in its interior.

Many of these latter are without rhyme or reason. Thus those who today explore its seemingly endless rooms and corridors frequently come on stairways that end in blank walls, doors that open outward into space, windows set into interior partitions, fireplaces without flues, intricate systems of bells and gongs and pushbuttons having no discoverable use, and much else of the same general nature; a veritable never-never land.

With building continuing six days a week for a period of thirty-eight years, and at no time following any ordered, over-all plan, the result was a truly fantastic structure, one that is said to contain well over a mile of corridors, windows to the number of 10,000, more than 2,000 doors, plus uncounted rooms of all sizes and shapes. Adding to the over-all confusion is the fact that in a number of instances smaller chambers have been constructed within the walls of larger ones, impressively designed doorways open into small closets, and in many of the apartments parts of the walls, ceilings, and floors are handsomely finished in rare woods, while in the remaining space only rough boards or crudely applied lath and plaster are visible. All in all, a truly weird Alice-in-Wonderland type of building; it is not surprising that for years it had been known to residents of the Santa Clara Valley as the Winchester House of Mystery.

Quite different from the fantastic Winchester House is that of another former resident of the San Jose area, Captain Charles M. Weber, a native of Germany who arrived in the province as a member of the Bidwell-Bartleson party in 1841. Weber settled first at the pueblo of San Jose; then, having been attracted by the fertile, tree-covered lands of the upper San Joaquin Valley, he and a partner, William Gulnap, acquired extensive holdings there from the Mexican authorities. Shortly thereafter, in 1845, Gulnap sold his half-interest in their 50,000-acre estate to Weber. According to legend, his compensation was $80, the amount of a grocery bill he owed his partner.

In 1847 Weber laid out a town on the banks of what is now Stockton Channel, which became known as Tuleberg. The settlement grew slowly at first and when gold was discovered the following year its founder joined in the rush to the Sierra diggings, prospecting along the banks of Weber Creek in Eldorado County. Soon, however, the migration to the goldfields having reached full tide, he abandoned mining and returned to Tuleberg, which by then was an important stopping place on the route to the southern mines, and devoted himself to supplying the needs of the newcomers.

Early in 1849 Weber had his town site resurveyed and at that time rechristened it Stockton in honor of Commodore Robert F. Stockton, the United States naval officer who had played an important part in the conquest of the provinces three years earlier. The settlement grew by leaps and bounds. Its population passed the 1,000 mark the following summer and for many months thereafter its newly laid-out streets were thronged day and night by hordes of Argonauts passing to and from the diggings.

180

75.   Weber House, Stockton.   Founder of the city of Stockton,
Captain Charles M. Weber put up the handsome residence —
shown above — in the early 1850s.   Destroyed by fire in 1881,
it was promptly rebuilt.   Later this second structure was moved
to a new site just outside the city limits, where it is still occupied
by a descendant of the original owner.   *Photograph by V. Covert
Martin, Stockton*

76. A California Parlor of the 1860s, Stockton.   One of the
features of Stockton's Pioneer Historical Museum are a number
of rooms depicting the domestic arrangements of Californians
of an earlier day.   This view shows a typical parlor during
Civil War times.   *Photograph by V. Covert Martin, Stockton*

PART IV: THE AGE OF THE MOGULS

The founder's first house was a small adobe which stood on a promontory beside the channel that has since been known as Weber Point. In 1851 this was replaced by a substantial, two-story wooden structure, the lumber and furnishings for which were brought round the Horn. For the next two decades, until Captain Weber's death in 1881, the house and the handsome gardens that surrounded it were well known to travelers who passed that way, the generous hospitality dispensed by its owner having become traditional.

When this building presently burned to the ground, a second impressive residence was built close by. Here Weber's descendants lived for many years; then, the district in which it stood having been taken over by docks, warehouses, and industrial plants, the big wooden residence was moved to a new site: an extensive, oak-studded area facing West Lane at the edge of town. There the picturesque, rambling house, its furnishings and decór making it a vertiable museum of the domestic elegance of a bygone age, is presided over by a descendant of the original Charles Weber.

One of the most interesting and best preserved southern California residences dating from Civil War days is the Phineas Banning home which, with its spacious grounds, was acquired by the city of Los Angeles in 1927 and is now known as Banning Park, a favorite recreation spot that lies in the southern part of that wide-spreading metropolis.

Built in 1864 by a wealthy pioneer resident of the district, the big, thirty-room frame house, patterned after the colonial mansions of his native Delaware, has as its most notable architectural feature an observation tower and "widow's walk" atop its roof, to which Banning used to climb and keep watch over his extensive interests in that area. For he was long a potent factor in the commercial and industrial development of the southland. In 1859 he founded a settlement on the coast to the south of Los Angeles, naming it Wilmington after the Delaware city where he was born.

77. Banning House, Wilmington. Long the home of Phineas Banning, operator of numerous stage lines throughout southern California in the early days, this handsome Colonial residence stands in the midst of a 20-acre recreation area known as Banning Park. In the old stables nearby are to be seen a stagecoach, carriages, and other vehicles of the pre-automobile age. *Photograph from the Title Insurance & Trust Co., Los Angeles*

PART IV: THE AGE OF THE MOGULS

There he constructed a pier and other facilities, thus making the town a regular port of call for the numerous freight and passenger vessels then engaged in the coast-wise trade. There, too, he established a carriage factory, and the vehicles turned out there, both wagons and smart buggies and surries, were a familiar sight on southern California roads prior to the advent of the horseless carriage. Transportation was long one of Banning's major interests and it was he who, in 1868, built the first railroad in the southern part of the state. This pioneer line is credited with having been instrumental in bringing the Southern Pacific to Los Angeles some ten years later, thereby linking up that city with the eastern seaboard.

No less interesting than the Banning House itself are the gardens that surround it. The huge, eighty-year-old eucalyptus tree that stands to the west of its main driveway is said to have been the first of that species to be planted in California, the forerunner of innumerable others to be found today in virtually every part of the state. To the rear of the house is a venerable wistaria vine, its branches, supported by an arbor, covering an area 200 feet from edge to edge. There each spring, when it is in the height of its bloom, it is the main attraction of a Western Festival, during which thousands visit the spot, both to admire the great vine and to be conducted through the mansion by a corps of pretty girls dressed in the picturesque costumes of pioneer days.

In the final decades of the last century one of the largest landowners in the southern half of the state was E. J. "Lucky" Baldwin. Having, as stated earlier, amassed a fortune from the fabulously rich silver mines on Nevada's Comstock Lode, he proceeded to enchance it through shrewd investments in lands adjacent to Los Angeles, which town then was just beginning its rocketlike growth. One of his purchases was the 13,000-acre Santa Anita Rancho, which lay east of Pasadena and south of Sierra Madre; this he acquired in 1875.

There he presently went to live, putting its fields under cultivation, setting out extensive orchards and vineyards, building a picturesque artificial lake, and on its shore erecting the ornate Queen Anne Cottage which still stands. Horse racing was long a major Baldwin enthusiasm, and at Santa Anita he established a breeding farm that produced many champions of the turf. The stables in which these thoroughbreds were housed were handsomely fitted out, with the stalls finished in rare woods and with profusion of millwork and wrought iron ornamenting their exteriors.

His own house, for all its designation as a "cottage," was on a scale hardly less elaborate. Built in the then popular Queen Anne style, its wide porches overlooking the lake on one side and a broad expanse of lawns on the other, its most striking feature is a tower three stories in height, to the top of which Baldwin used to pilot his guests to admire the wide view it afforded of the surrounding countryside — a view that is now much restricted due to the growth of the trees of its garden. Within, the house is finished in the best manner of the period, the ground floor rooms replete with carved stone fireplaces, black walnut woodwork, marble floors, and intricately designed stained glass windows. Its original furnishings — all in the Queen Anne style — are said to have been purchased by Baldwin from that on display at the Philadelphia Centennial Exposition of 1876, to which he was a visitor.

Following the owner's death in 1909, the house long stood vacant; its furniture was removed and scattered, and the building itself fell into disrepair. Meantime the big Santa Anita Rancho was broken up and sold, and in the mid-1920s the 140-acre piece that included the old house and its grounds was taken over by the Los Angeles State and County Arboretum, which has there assembled some 40,000 plants indigenous to California.

Some years later a group of volunteers, terming themselves the Arboretum Historical Committee, was formed, taking as its first objective the rehabilitation of the Queen Anne Cottage and the area surrounding it. This project has since been carried out in admirable fashion. The

78. Baldwin Cottage, Santa Anita. This quaint little Queen
Anne cottage, surmounted by its ornate tower, was put up by
E. J. "Lucky" Baldwin, Comstock millionaire, shortly after,
in 1875, he purchased the big Santa Anita Rancho to the east
of Los Angeles. Today half a dozen populous towns occupy
the lands where once roamed Baldwin's herds of cattle and
thoroughbred horses. *Photograph from the Los Angeles County*
Chamber of Commerce, Los Angeles

79. Jesse Shepard House, San Diego. Typical of the complex
domestic architecture of the Victorian period is this residence
which stands at the corner of 20th and **K** streets in San Diego.
Its builder and long-time resident was a musician of local note
and throughout the 1880s and 1890s many well-known figures
in the musical and theatrical world were entertained there.
Photograph from the Union Title Insurance & Trust Co., San Diego

gardens have been restored, complete with croquet court, winding paths, and flower beds set out to plants that grew there during Baldwin's day. The carriage house nearby has likewise been reconditioned and in it are displayed coaches, tally-hos, and other smart vehicles in which the original owner was wont to drive about his property.

Within the house itself, now restored to its pristine elegance, have been assembled, piece by piece, the furniture, bric-a-brac, and other fixtures characteristic of the period.

Another of the many ornate residences dating from the Victorian period that still stand in various parts of southern California is the Villa Montezuma at the corner of 20th and K streets in San Diego. Put up in the late 1880s by Jesse Shepard, a pianist and singer of considerable note, its chief architectural features include the lavish use of stained glass in windows and doors, and an elaborate tower, topped by a mosquelike cupola, that rises above its complex roof and from which a wide view of the bay and the surrounding countryside may be had.

Shepard, who was something of a mystic, always maintained that his Villa Montezuma had been built in accordance with instructions from the spirit world, his astral advisor being presumably Montezuma I, Emperor of the Aztecs. Despite that idiosyncrasy, however, he was highly regarded in musical circles during the final decade of the last century and the early years of the present. The frequent recitals and concerts held at the villa were always well attended by the townspeople, and it is said that few of the famous singers and musicians who reached San Diego during that period failed to partake of the hospitality dispensed at the picturesque villa.

PART

V

SHRINES AND SHOWPLACES

Scattered throughout the length of the state are a number of residences, some dating from the earliest days, others of comparatively recent origin, that for any one of a variety of reasons have come to be looked on as having a particular significance in the eyes of today's residents. Certain of these are revered because they were once the homes of men or women who made important contributions to the artistic or literary life of the region, or who were eminent in related fields of endeavor; others have stirred the imagination of the populace — or at any rate, aroused their curiosity — mainly by reason of their tremendous size and, in most cases, by the magnificence of the grounds that surround them.

Facing one of the tree-lined streets of Red Bluff, a quiet river town near the northern end of the Sacramento Valley, stands a little house belonging in the first of these categories; namely, a modest frame residence that was once known to thousands in all parts of the nation. This is the John Brown Cottage where for a period of six years beginning in 1864, lived the widow and several of the children of the famed abolitionist. The little building, its outlines somewhat altered by later additions, is located on the west side of Main Street, near the southern boundary of the town.

The story of how Mrs. Brown and her three daughters came to live there is a curious and interesting one. John Brown's visionary plan for liberating the slaves, a plan that resulted in his forcible capture of the United States Armory at Harpers Ferry in 1859, followed by his long-drawn-out trial on the charge of leading an armed insurrection and his subsequent execution, had made him a martyr in the eyes of the abolitionists all over the land.

Following the outbreak of the Civil War, that feeling was intensified and when, in 1863, word reached Red Bluff that his widow was homeless and in want, a group of citizens launched a campaign to provide her with a house and have her come out and live among them. This humane project was widely publicized in the California newspapers of the day and contributions poured in from every corner of the state, with the result that not only was the little cottage on Main Street built and presented to her but, in addition, she was given a considerable sum of cash.

She and her daughters remained there until 1870, then she sold the house and went to live at a spot closer to the ocean in nearby Humboldt County. It is said that the reason for this move was that the elderly woman, who was in bad health, found the summer heat of the valley oppressive and her doctors advised that she seek a cooler climate. In any event, the little wooden house, with its single gable in front and its steep-pitched shingle roof, has ever since been pointed out by Red Bluff residents as one of the historic landmarks of their town, a monument to the public spirit and practical generosity of their forebears more than nine decades ago.

A decade later, in 1881, Brown's widow made yet another move, this time farther down the coast to Santa Clara County. There on

80. John Brown Cottage, Red Bluff. This simple little dwelling, standing near the southern end of this valley town's Main Street, was presented by the citizens of Red Bluff to the widow of the noted abolitionist. There she and her three daughters lived from 1864 to 1870. *Photograph from the California State Library, Sacramento*

81. Luther Burbank Home, Santa Rosa. Here on the grounds surrounding his residence close to the present center of the town, and on his "Experimental Farm" at nearby Sebastopol, Luther Burbank for more than fifty years conducted his experiments designed to improve the quality of fruits, flowers, and vegetables. Among his productions, now widely grown all over the nation, are the Burbank potato, the Shasta daisy, the thornless cactus, and literally scores of others. *Photograph by Keith's Studio, Santa Rosa*

a picturesque bit of wooded property in the hills behind Saratoga, she lived the final three years of her long life, virtually forgotten by the world at large but still an object of veneration to some as the relict of the martyred Brown. It was a group of the latter, most of whom lived in or about San Jose, who presented her with this, her third California home, paying a reported $1850 for it, together with the twenty acres of wooded hillsides that comprised the "ranch." Long known as the John Brown Lodge, the little structure stands on an elevated spot from which a wide view may be had of the Santa Clara Valley below: a two-story frame cottage with spacious porches at both the first and second floor levels, its white paint causes it to stand out sharply against a row of cypress trees in the rear.

In the town of Santa Rosa, some fifty miles to the north of San Francisco, is to be seen the house and experimental gardens of the eminent horticulturist, Luther Burbank, whose experiments in the propagation of plant life resulted in the development of numerous new and improved varieties of plants, fruits and flowers. His property there, now known as the Luther Burbank House and Gardens, stands at the corner of Santa Rosa Avenue and Tupper Street, only a block or two from the center of town. Following Burbank's death in 1926, it was presented by his widow to the Santa Rosa Junior College, and it has since been under the care of the college's Department of Botany. It is open to the public and each year attracts many thousands of visitors.

Burbank, born in Lancaster, Massachusetts, in 1849, located in the fertile Santa Rosa Valley while in his mid-twenties. Thereafter for more than half a century he conducted his plant experiments, both in the gardens surrounding his Santa Rosa home and in an extensive plot of land just west of the neighboring town of Sebastopol. The most widely known of his productions are the Burbank potato, the Shasta daisy, and the spineless cactus, but he was responsible, too, for improved varieties of numerous other fruits, berries, and vegetables. Upon his

82. Fountain Grove, near Santa Rosa. Relic of one of the numerous co-operative colonies established in various parts of California during the final third of the last century, this residence served as the headquarters of the Fountain Grove group. It stands, surrounded by extensive vineyards set out by the colonists, a few miles north of Santa Rosa. *Photograph by Norman Miner, Santa Rosa*

death, at the age of seventy-seven, he was buried beneath a tall deodar tree on the grounds of his Santa Rosa estate.

His residence there, a comfortable but unpretentious two-story structure, set back from the street and half hidden by trees and shrubbery he himself had planted, and on which he conducted many of his most productive experiments, is daily open to visitors between the hours of 10 A.M. and 4 P.M.

At a number of spots throughout the state there are to be seen visual reminders of certain once widely publicized experiments in communal living that were carried out during the early days. Ventures of that sort, in which each member of the group had, in theory at least, an equal voice in the management of the affairs of the community, and where all property was held in common, were fairly common all over the nation throughout the second half of the last century.

These colonies differed widely, not only in size and degree of prosperity, but in the purpose that had drawn the members together. With some the reason was purely economic, as in the case of the Anaheim Colony, described later in this chapter. The majority, however, were planned either as practical applications of the socialistic doctrines then widely current both in Europe and the western part of the United States, or as retreats where members of certain religious cults could follow the tenets of their faith free from outside interference.

One of the most curious — and interesting — of these last-named groups was that which founded, and long maintained, the Fountain Grove Colony in Sonoma County, some two miles to the north of Santa Rosa. The founder of this community and throughout the twenty-odd years of its existence its leader in all things, was Thomas Lake Harris, a religious mystic born in England, who, after some years as a Universalist preacher, broke away from that faith and launched a sect which he called the Brotherhood of the New Life. Gathering adherents, he established colonies throughout the 1860s and early 1870s at a number of places in New York State, then, in 1875, moved to California, bringing with him a group of followers.

The site he selected for his new colony lies in a pleasant valley among the foothills on the east side of the Santa Rosa plain. There, being plentifully supplied with funds — for one of the tenets of the creed was that those who joined must contribute all their wordly goods to the cause — he bought a tract of land comprising some 700 acres (later this was substantially increased) and began the construction of a group of buildings: houses to shelter the colonists, shops, barns for the livestock, and presently a substantial stone winery, for the growing of grapes and the making of wine and brandy were long the colony's major industry.

The first building to be completed was Harris' own home, which he called "Aestivossa." This — which still stands — is a handsome building following what was described at the time as the Adams-Georgian style of architecture. Two stories high, the ground floor contains spacious parlors, a library, and dining room, all tastefully finished with paneled walls and opening onto a broad veranda on one side and a glassed-in sunroom on the other, while the second floor and attic were given over to commodious bedrooms. At the time of its building, and for years thereafter, the "Harris Mansion" was one of the show-places of the region, possessing as it did such elegancies as stained glass windows, running water and marble washstands in the major bedrooms, and—greatest wonder of all—being illuminated by gas made on the premises.

Fountain Grove prospered for some fifteen years; then, like most other such utopian schemes, dissension from within, combined with suspicion on the part of conventionally minded residents of neighboring communities, began to have its effect. In 1892, Harris, wearying, it is said, of quarrels within the fold and the growing hostility of the California press — which by then was accusing the members of all manner of religious heresies and moral lapses — left the colony and returned to the east coast. Those left behind continued the experiment for some years longer, but the communal principles on which it had

83.   Ruins of Jack London's Wolf House, Glen Ellen.   These melancholy stone walls are all that remain of the handsome house London built on his ranch in the upper Sonoma Valley and which was destroyed by fire a few days before he was to move in.   His plan to rebuild it was prevented by his death in 1916, at the age of forty.   *Photograph by Keith's Studio, Santa Rosa*

been founded gradually went into the discard and in 1900 the property passed to private ownership. Today the imposing residence of its leader and the picturesque stone building that once housed Fountain Grove Winery are virtually the only reminders of the once flourishing community established there by members of the Brotherhood of the New Life.

Some fifteen miles to the southeast of Fountain Grove stands one of the most widely known of California residences — one that, paradoxically, has never been lived in. Moreover, despite its renown in places far beyond the borders of the state, only a comparatively few have ever laid eyes on it, and these latter have seen nothing more than an assemblage of masonry walls, its doors and windows vacant, its once spacious rooms open to the sky. For these are all that remain of Wolf House, the big stone castle Jack London caused to be built on his extensive Glen Ellen ranch, and where he hoped to live and work and entertain his friends for many years to come.

This was a hope that was never fulfilled. For when, after months of planning, and two solid years of construction, Wolf House at last stood complete and its proud owner was making ready to move in, fire broke out on the night of August 18, 1913, and, raging uncontrolled — for no water was available to fight it — by daylight had reduced the big structure to smoking ruin.

To London, who had stood helplessly by throughout the night, the blow was a severe one, for into its building had gone not only his hopes but a major part of his earnings during the previous two years. Nonetheless he promptly began laying plans for its rebuilding, having the ashes and rubble cleared from the site and giving orders for the felling of a nearby grove of redwood trees to provide lumber for the interior: studding and joists for the floors and partitions, paneling for London's combination workroom and sleeping quarters, hand-hewn beams for the ceiling of the social hall on the ground floor of the big, three-story house, and much else.

200

PART V: SHRINES AND SHOWPLACES

As it eventuated, however, Wolf House was never rebuilt. For although at the time of its burning London was but thirty-seven years old, yet he had crowded so much activity into that period that the fires of his inspiration were already seeming to burn less brightly. Plans to begin the actual reconstruction were put off from month to month and at length were abandoned entirely. A year or two later, in the fall of 1916, the owner was dead, being then only a few months past his fortieth birthday.

Today the ruins of Wolf House stand in melancholy isolation on their wooded knoll overlooking the peaceful fields and meadows that comprise the upper end of the Sonoma Valley, its walls, fashioned from the native stone, already weathered to mellow tones by the action of sun and rain, and the whole slowly taking on the aspect of another and more romantic age than our own.

Long noted as a center for the production of fine wines is the Napa Valley, which lies to the north of San Francisco Bay, rimmed in by rolling, wooded hills to the east and west and with the 4,343-foot bulk of Mount Saint Helena lying athwart its northern end. The first vine-yards were set out in the area more than a century ago, and by 1880 thousands of acres of the valley floor and the adjacent foothills were planted to the vines. Half a dozen wineries were then in operation, producing a variety of light table wines that were already finding favor all over the nation.

In that year, 1880, Robert Louis Stevenson, spending his honey-moon at an abandoned quicksilver mine on a flank of Mount Saint Helena, became much interested in this new industry that had sprung up in the valley below. In *Silverado Squatters* he records a visit to one of the pioneer establishments, that of a German ex-barber named Jacob Schram, who had acquired the property in 1862, set out his hillside vineyards, built a big house and stone winery, and hired a crew of Chinese coolies to drive a series of tunnels into the hillside to serve as storage cellars. Stevenson, himself no mean judge of wines, found that his host's products, which were marketed under the trade name of "Schramsberger," were in no wise inferior to similar wines then being produced in France.

Schram's winery — which, together with his commodious wooden residence, still stands — is located close to the town of Calistoga, at the upper end of the valley. A few miles farther to the south, in the vicinity of Saint Helena and Rutherford, are a number of other old-established wineries, some bearing names that are known to fanciers of good wines from coast to coast. Among these are Beringer Brothers, founded in 1876, Louis M. Martini, Beaulieu, Inglenook, and several others. Virtually all have been in business for seventy-five years or longer, and their wide-spreading vineyards, stone wineries, and attendant structures, together with the spacious homes of their owners, give the countryside an appearance not unlike that of the wine-producing centers of France and Germany.

One of the oldest and most picturesque of these properties is the Charles Krug Winery, a cluster of ivy-covered buildings that stand beside the highway a short distance to the north of the town of Saint Helena. Its founder was Charles Krug, a young emigrant from Germany, who, in 1858, bought a tract of land there and the following year produced, on a small, hand-operated cider press, what is said to have been the first wine made in the valley. During the years that followed, and until his death in 1894, Krug closely supervised every detail of the operation, from the selection of the vines to be planted to the successive steps of the manufacturing and aging process, with the result that throughout this period the Krug vintages won a high place for themselves among discriminating fanciers of light table wines.

Upon the founder's passing, the property was purchased by James K. Moffitt, San Francisco banker, who used the handsome Krug house and its gardens for a summer home, meantime leasing the vineyards and winery to others. This arrangement continued until the advent of prohibition, whereupon winemaking was suspended. In 1943, how-

84. Stone Cottage, Asti Winery, near Cloverdale. California wineries, particularly those in the Santa Rosa, Sonoma, and Napa valleys, exhibit many interesting examples of the architecture of bygone days. Above is the superintendent's house at Asti, put up soon after the Italian-Swiss colony was established there in 1881. *Photograph by Norman Miner, Santa Rosa*

ever, the estate passed to new owners and operations were resumed; today the Krug name once more occupies an honored place among the makers of fine California wines.

In the town of Napa, a short distance to the south of Saint Helena, stands one of the choicest surviving examples of the country homes put up by wealthy Californians during the latter third of the last century. This is Oak Knoll, built in the late 1870s by "Hank" Woodward, an elaborate frame structure replete with the towers, gables, dormers, and ornate millwork characteristic of the period.

Woodward was an early San Franciscan, with a notable flair for showmanship. This was first manifested in the latter 1850s when he operated one of the town's pioneer hostelries, the What Cheer House on Leidesdorff Street. For, in addition to providing his guests with rooms and meals, he offered attractions virtually unknown in the hotels of the day. Among these were not only a well-stocked library and reading room, but what he termed a museum, the latter containing a collection of stuffed animals, specimens of the prodigiously big fruits and vegetables grown in California's fertile soil (including a potato 30 inches long and said to weigh 12 1/2 pounds), and a variety of other interest-provoking curios.

This, however, was only the beginning. By the early 1870's the extensive grounds about Woodward's residence on Mission Street had been converted into an amusement park and for the next two decades it remained a favorite gathering place for San Franciscans on pleasure bent. For Woodward's Gardens offered attractions to suit virtually every taste: for the serious-minded, an art gallery, conservatory, zoo, and aquarium, with attendants on hand to explain the wonders they contained; for those seeking entertainment, there were daily band concerts and nightly balls, along with frequent special attractions in the form of balloon ascensions, troupes of tightwalk performers, and elaborate fireworks displays; while for the children there were boat

85. John Muir Home, near Martinez. Standing atop a knoll and commanding a view of the wooded Alhambra Valley, this commodious frame structure was long the home of the famous naturalist; John Muir (1838–1914), author of *The Mountains of California* and numerous other works.   *Photograph by Harry W. Abrahams, San Francisco*

rides on a miniature lake, thrilling trips on the back of a camel, a merry-go-round, and much else. All this was for a modest admission charge of twenty-five cents. So popular did the resort become that its owner several times had to enlarge it; eventually it occupied two full city blocks, connected by a tunnel passing beneath Fourteenth Street.

That the Gardens returned its owner a handsome profit is indicated by the elaborate summer home he put up in the Napa Valley sometime prior to 1880. Standing on a slight eminence and surrounded by a stately grove of oaks — hence, its name, Oak Knoll — its square central tower, rising above two floors of spacious, high-ceilinged rooms, commands a sweeping view of the pretty valley and its frame of wooded, gently rolling hills.

On the crest of a hill, back a little distance from the winding Franklin Canyon road that leads westward from the town of Martinez, stands a square, two-story residence, its white walls and red roof rising above the greenery of its garden and surrounding orchards and vineyards. The structure, surmounted by a bewindowed cupola on the apex of its roof, is of no particular distinction architecturally, it being more or less typical of scores of other houses put up by moderately prosperous California ranchers during the 1870s and later. Yet it has gained a renown that extends far beyond its immediate vicinity and annually attracts a quota of interested visitors.

For it was long the home of John Muir, the amiable Scotch naturalist, explorer, and publicist, whose many magazine articles and books, notably his *Mountains of California*, served to spread abroad an appreciation of the scenic wonders of the far west. For several decades prior to his death in 1914, Muir lived at this little Martinez estate during the intervals between his protracted field trips: to the remoter parts of the high Sierra country, to Mexico, Alaska, and elsewhere.

The story of how this far-ranging naturalist came to settle in this prim Martinez ranch house, and there spend his remaining days, is an interesting one. The man who built the house was a Polish doctor named John Strentzel, who had reached this country in 1840, joined one of the pioneer emigrant trains to California some years later, and, after sundry adventures in the goldfields, purchased the little Alhambra Valley rancho in the middle 1850s. There the doctor attended the ailing among the early settlers of the area, raised his family, and set out his orchard and vineyard. He was an ardent horticulturist and the fruits he raised on his fertile acres presently began to win prizes at the Sacramento State Fair for their superior size and flavor.

It was in order to inspect Strentzel's vines and trees and growing methods that young Muir first visited the spot. But what drew him back again and again was not the doctor's prize-winning apples and grapes and berries, but his comely young daughter. A romance presently developed between the pair; they were married in the late 1880s, lived for a time in a cottage on the property and then, following Strentzel's death in 1890, moved into the house on the hill.

This remained Muir's home for close to a quarter century; there his children were born, and there, his wife having presently died, he spent the years of his widowerhood, writing his books and articles in one of the second-floor corner rooms which he had converted into a study. Callers who made their way into that big, book-lined chamber during Muir's later years have stated that the scene it presented might have come straight out of a Dickens novel. Disordered masses of papers covered the top of the writing desk; stacks of books and magazines — the overflow from the crowded shelves — occupied the chairs and tables or were deposited in heaps on the floor, and a jumble of photographs, curios gathered on his field trips, and assorted bits of memorabilia stood on the mantel above the fireplace or were stuck into the frames of pictures on the walls. All were covered with months-long accumulations of dust and grime, for Muir would brook no efforts on the part of his Chinese houseboy to "tidy up," claiming that he knew exactly where to put his hands on anything he wanted.

The property is still owned by Muir's descendants and is normally closed to visitors. However, from time to time, proposals have been made that it be incorporated into the state park system and so opened to the public as a literary shrine honoring the memory of the genial naturalist who was long known to his friends as "John of the Mountains."

High in the hills behind Oakland and commanding a sweeping view of San Francisco Bay stands another literary shrine — this one a picturesque little building that for close to three quarters of a century has been renowned throughout California and farther afield. For from the mid-1880s until 1913 this was the home of Joaquin Miller, the colorful "Poet of the Sierras," many of whose poems — particularly his eulogies of Lincoln and Columbus — were widely known and quoted by a bygone generation.

Born in Ohio in 1841 and christened Cincinnatus Heine Miller, he was taken as a child to Oregon Territory and spent his youth and young manhood on the Western frontier, living for a time with the Modoc Indians in northern California. During that period he discarded his given name of Cincinnatus in favor of Joaquin; this, so he later claimed, was in honor of the half-legendary early-date bandit, Joaquin Murieta. In the middle 1870s, having published a volume of verses and written several plays — one of which, *The Danites of the Sierras*, attained a widespread popularity — he went to England where for several seasons his informal manners and colorful frontier costumes made him a darling of the London drawing rooms.

Miller bought "The Hights," as he insisted on spelling it, in 1886, and at once set about building a home there. Having a deep-seated scorn of the conventional in all things, his house had of course to differ radically from the common run. It was in fact three buildings, each containing a single room, placed end to end, their floors at different levels, and with the steep-pitched roof of each unit terminating in a

86. Joaquin Miller's The Hights, Oakland. Long one of the most picturesque of California's literary figures was Joaquin Miller, the "Poet of the Sierras." Shown here is the group of cottages known as The Hights (as he insisted on spelling it), long a favorite gathering place for the literati of the area.
Photograph from the Oakland Public Library, Oakland

central peak. This abode he termed "The Abbey," some say in tribute to his third wife, the former Abbie Leland (who long refused to live there), and others that it was named after an English country house, Newstead Abbey, where he had once been a guest.

When "The Abbey" was finished Miller set about making further improvements on his seventy-acre hilltop estate. One of his pet projects was the setting out of thousands of young trees: eucalypti, cypresses, pines, and acacias, which today cover the once-barren hillsides with a mass of greenery. Another was the building of a group of curious stone monuments, tributes to three eminent — but widely dissimilar — personages for whom he professed deep admiration; namely, the prophet Moses, Robert Browning, and John C. Frémont. In the erecting of these shrines he sometimes pressed into service certain young writers who were frequent visitors to "The Hights," a group that included George Sterling, Jack London, Herman Scheffauer, Edwin Markham, and a young Japanese poet named Yone Noguchi.

While putting up yet another of his monuments, however, he would accept no outside help, preferring to build it entirely with his own hands. This was a stone platform which stands a bit higher up the hill from "The Abbey," and which he intended as his own funeral pyre, leaving orders that his body be cremated there and his ashes scattered by the winds. By the time of his death in 1913, however, "The Hights" had become a part of Oakland and it was discovered that a city ordinance prohibited such informal cremations; so that wish went unrealized.

In 1917 the estate was purchased by the city of Oakland and today is known as Joaquin Miller Park, a favorite picnic ground for residents of the area. "The Abbey" still stands and is normally open to visitors interested in examining the desk, manuscripts, and other mementos of the colorful "Poet of the Sierras" that are on display there.

In one of San Francisco's residential districts, at the corner of Filbert and Webster streets, is to be seen a bizarre structure that, built in the early 1900s, has ever since been an object of wonder to passersby. Be-

87. Hindu Temple, San Francisco. This curious structure,
standing at the corner of Filbert and Webster streets, serves
both as a residence and as a place of worship. Built in 1904
as a gathering place for those of the Hindu faith, a chapel and
auditorium occupy the ground floor while its roof is surmounted by a group of towers and minarets said to be of
Gothic, Hindu, Shiva, and Moslem design.   *Photograph from
the California Historical Society, San Francisco*

88. Stevenson House, Monterey. Here Robert Louis Stevenson, then unknown to fame and in miserable health, lived for several months in 1879, prior to his marriage to Fanny Osbourne. *Photograph by Moulin Studios, San Francisco*

cause no name or other means of identification appears on its exterior, few are aware of its true nature or of the meaning of its extraordinarily complex architecture. Its first two stories differ but little from the usual domestic architecture of the period, the second-floor rooms having the sun-catching bay windows common to most San Francisco residences of half a century ago, the one unusual feature being the pointed designs above the windows of the ground floor, which give the lower story an unexpected suggestion of the Far East.

It is, however, the third floor that catches and holds the eye, frequently bringing those who come upon the building for the first time to a complete halt. For perched atop this otherwise by no means extraordinary dwelling is a complex aggregation of towers, minarets, and colonnades of various sizes and shapes, each of which has a symbolic meaning to those of the Moslem faith. The structure has long been the headquarters of the Vedanta Society, and the place of worship for members of that cult in the San Francisco Bay region. As such it lends yet another exotic touch to the skyline of that cosmopolitan city.

In Monterey, on Houston Street, between Pearl and Webster, stands a white-plastered adobe building that has long been an object of veneration to townspeople and visitors alike. For this is the Robert Louis Stevenson House, to which the frail Scot, then virtually unknown and in wretched health, came in the fall of 1879, and as such it is regarded as the town's foremost literary shrine.

To be sure, Stevenson's stay there was brief, he having reached the Monterey peninsula in late September of that year and left it less than three months later. The romantic errand that had drawn him all the way from his native Edinburgh to this indolent early California village is, of course, well known. It was to join his ladylove, Fanny Van de Grift Osbourne, whom he had met the previous year at an artists' colony outside Paris and whom, following her divorce from her husband, Sam Osbourne, he presently married.

Stevenson took up quarters in the big, draughty building, then operated as a sailors' lodging house and known as the French Hotel, on the recommendation of one of his new-found friends, Jules Simoneau, a French emigré who was currently conducting a restaurant on the same street. Precisely what room — or rooms — he occupied during the weeks of his sojourn has long been a subject of debate, for Stevenson's own references to the matter but add to the confusion. Thus, in one of his letters to his London friend and literary advisor, Sidney Colvin, he makes allusion to "my airy rooms with five windows commanding a view of the bay," a statement that can only come under the heading of literary license since it does violence both to the location and architecture of the structure.

At any rate, his stay was far from idle, for there he spent many hours daily, much of the time propped up in bed, while he wrote *The Amateur Emigrant*, that high-spirited account of his trip across the continent with a trainload of impoverished settlers, mostly new arrivals from various countries of Europe, and there, too, he produced an essay on Thoreau and a piece of fiction called *The Vendetta of the West*.

The Stevenson House, as it has long been known, is kept in excellent repair by its present owners. A plaque affixed to its front makes known its literary associations, and from time to time movements, sponsored by public-spirited local groups, have been launched to have it preserved as a permanent memorial to the gentle Scotch romancer who made it his abode.

What has often been termed the most imposing — and costly — private residence within the confines of the state is the big San Simeon castle owned by newspaper publisher William Randolph Hearst, which stands in lonely solitude atop La Cuesta Encantada (i.e., "The Enchanted Hill") on the rugged coast some fifty miles to the north of San Luis Obispo. Commanding a wide view of the ocean on one side and the high, wooded summits of the Santa Lucia Range on the other, it has a setting no less spectacular than the cluster of towers, turrets, buttresses, and baronial halls that constitute the castle itself.

89. Stevenson's Room, Monterey. This is said to be the room occupied by the Scotch writer in the fall of 1879 and where, between sieges of illness, he composed much of *The Amateur Emigrant* and *The Vendetta of the West*. *Photograph by Lee Blaisdell, Monterey*

90. Hearst's "Enchanted Hill" San Simeon. One of the west coast's most remarkable residences is this country seat of the late newspaper publisher, which stands facing the Pacific above the village of San Simeon, about fifty miles to the north of San Luis Obispo. Called La Cuesta Encantada ("The Enchanted Hill"), it consists of the main castle, surrounded by no less than four large guest houses, three of the latter replicas of French chateaux. Since Hearst's death the big estate has remained untenanted save for a crew of caretakers. *Photograph by Wide World, New York*

PART V: SHRINES AND SHOWPLACES

The estate, embracing scores of square miles of virgin territory extending from the seacoast to beyond the crests of the mountains, was originally owned by the publisher's father, Senator George Hearst, who acquired it in the early 1880s. There, close to the village of San Simeon — which in the early days had been a whaling station — he built a comfortable farmhouse to which he retired for a few weeks each summer. Following the Senator's death in 1891 the property passed to his son William who, for the next two decades was so engrossed in the building of his newspaper empire that he rarely visited the spot.

Then, about 1912, on a hilltop some five miles back from the ocean, he began the construction of his fabulous castle. Its building went on for years, for hardly was one unit completed before work began on the next. Today the estate, which from a distance resembles a fortified hill village of medieval times, consists of the great main house — La Casa Grande — surrounded by four guest houses, the first with the massive walls and towers suggestive of fifteenth century Spanish architecture, and the others patterned after French chateaux. Included in the main building is a commodious theater, and on the grounds are tennis courts, a swimming pool, a once well-stocked zoo, and, on the plain below, a private flying field for the use of guests who chose to arrive by air.

For years Hearst and his agents ransacked Europe and the Orient for art objects and other materials designed to beautify the San Simeon estate. Entire castles were purchased, torn down stone by stone and reassembled on the hilltop. Paintings, statues, and tapestries in prodigious quantities were bought to ornament the halls and galleries of the main house and its attendant structures, and boatloads of antique chests, tables, chairs, and carpets were used to furnish the hundreds of rooms. So large were his purchases that two big warehouses were built in the village in which to store new shipments until places could be found for them on the hill, and on Hearst's death in 1951, these were filled to capacity.

91. Scotty's Castle, Death Valley. Near the northern edge
of the Death Valley National Monument and close to the
California-Nevada line stands the handsome Spanish Provincial hacienda that was once one of the most widely publicized residences in the nation. For here lived the mysterious
Death Valley Scotty, whose picturesque stunts were widely
heralded in the newspapers from coast to coast. Not until
years later was it learned that the money he spent so freely
was provided by a Chicago friend, Albert M. Johnson.
Photograph by Dave Packwood, Los Angeles

Since then the castle has for the most part remained untenanted save for a crew of caretakers who patrol the houses and grounds on guard against fires or trespassers. Recently the proposal has been made that the property be taken over by the state and opened to the public as a part of the California park system. However, legislation to that effect has not yet been enacted, and meanwhile the ornate gates to the castle remain padlocked.

Another widely publicized home within the confines of the state is the huge tile and concrete building known as Scotty's Castle, which stands in lonely grandeur, surrounded by many miles of desolation, near the northern boundary of the Death Valley National Monument. The castle, a big, rambling structure replete with the towers, arcades, and patios characteristic of Spanish provincial architecture, was built in the early 1920s, at an estimated cost of $2,000,000. The man who was its purported owner, and who was to live in it until his death more than two decades later, was a picturesque individual known all over the west as Death Valley Scotty.

Scotty — his true name was Walter A. Scott — was always something of a mystery even to those who knew him well, for he was ever chary of revealing information concerning his background. Seemingly a typical desert prospector, he first came to public attention in 1905 when he appeared one day in Los Angeles, possessed of a seemingly limitless supply of money which he proceeded to squander in a variety of spectacular ways. The most notable of his stunts on that occasion was to charter a special train in which he made a record-breaking, forty-five-hour run to Chicago.

For years it was Scotty's contention that the source of his wealth was a secret gold mine hidden away in one of the arid canyons of the Valley, and many were those who sought unavailingly to locate the bonanza. Not until near the end of his life was it revealed that the man who financed his picturesque exploits was a Chicago millionaire, one

Albert M. Johnson, who seems to have thoroughly enjoyed Scotty's place in the limelight while himself remaining discreetly in the background.

In any event there was apparently no limit to the benefactor's generosity. For the castle — in reality it is a cluster of buildings grouped about a central patio and joined by covered porticos — was, and remains, an authentic showplace, its interior replete with imported tiling, hand-carved woodwork, and other elegant — and expensive — appointments. All this is the more surprising when it is considered that it stands in the midst of one of the most desolate and sparsely settled regions in the entire nation, and that virtually all the material that went into its construction and furnishing had to be transported over many miles of sandy desert roads.

Following Scotty's death in 1954, the castle was converted into a hotel and museum, and now each season groups of guests occupy its spacious bedrooms and gather on its patio enjoying the Valley's salubrious winter climate.

In the town of Anaheim, on the banks of the Santa Ana River some twenty-eight miles to the southeast of Los Angeles, at the corner of West and Sycamore streets, is to be seen a neat little frame cottage that annually attracts many visitors, particularly those interested in the early history of the state. For it was the first house to be erected in the Anaheim Colony, one of the earliest of a number of experiments in communal living launched in California during the early days. This group, made up largely of German emigrants residing in San Francisco, banded together in 1857 and purchased an 1100-acre tract of fertile land on the north bank of the river. This was divided into twenty-acre farms and a certain area was set aside as a site for their village. The name chosen for the little community, Anaheim, was that of the river, combined with "heim," the German word for home.

From the beginning the colony flourished, its members setting out orchards and vineyards on their twenty-acre plots and establishing

92. Patio of Scotty's Castle. This separates the two main
units of the big house, the building of which is said to have
cost Scotty's silent backer close to $2,000,000. *Photograph by
Dave Packwood, Los Angeles*

93. Pioneer House, Anaheim. Relic of one of the numerous co-operative land colonies established in California in the early days, this prim little cottage was long the headquarters of the Anaheim group, numbering some fifty members of German descent, who settled there in 1857. Unlike most such experiments, the colony flourished and many descendants of the original members still live in the area. *Photograph from the Anaheim Chamber of Commerce, Anaheim*

a store, a church, a school, and other gathering places in the town. About the outer boundary of the property the settlers constructed a fence, using for that purpose great numbers of pickets freshly cut from the willow trees that grew along the banks of the river. Many thousands of these pickets took root, with the result that for years thereafter the lands of the colony were enclosed in a wall of living green.

Although the original members were an uncommonly varied group, including in their number merchants, blacksmiths, carpenters, a shoemaker, a miller, a brewer, a poet, and a musician, all were frugal and industrious, and they are said to have lived together in complete harmony, meantime bringing their lands to a high degree of productivity.

During the first three decades the growing of grapes and the making of wine were major industries; in the late 1880s, however, a blight destroyed many of the vineyards, whereupon the lands were set out to orange and walnut trees, which were then being widely planted throughout southern California. In the Anaheim region many of these original groves are still producing handsomely.

Pioneer House, the little structure at West and Sycamore streets — to which spot it was moved some years ago from its initial location — has been converted into a museum in which has been assembled a varied collection of relics brought to the colony by the early-day settlers: tables, chairs, musical instruments and other household furnishings, portraits, documents, old newspapers, and similar material. To present-day visitors, not the least interesting exhibit is the cottage itself. For from viewing its small, neat rooms, its wide porch extending across the front, and its tiny garden enclosed in a prim picket fence, one gains an excellent idea of what the farmhouses of the area were like a hundred years ago.

Lying some distance to the southwest of Los Angeles harbor is the island of Santa Catalina, a rugged area twenty miles long and eight miles across at its widest point. Catalina was discovered in 1542 by

94. Wrigley Mansion, Santa Catalina Island. On a hill above picturesque Avalon Bay and commanding a view of the town of that name stands the residence of chewing-gum magnate, William Wrigley, Jr., who, settling there in 1919, was primarily responsible for making Avalon the popular resort it is today. *Photograph from the Los Angeles County Chamber of Commerce, Los Angeles*

the Portuguese navigator, Juan Rodriguez Cabrillo, and was given its present name by Sebastian Vizcaino, who visited the spot sixty years later. For more than two centuries and a half thereafter the island was but little known to the outer world, its sole inhabitants during most of that period being a tribe of Indians who gained a precarious livelihood by trapping birds that nested there and by fish caught in the water offshore.

Then, in the mid-1860s, the finding of traces of gold at several spots set off a miniature stampede to the island and the staking out of hundreds of claims. However, no strikes of importance were made and after a few months the excitement subsided and Catalina once more lapsed into somnolence. Finally, in the 1890s and early 1900s, a number of attempts were made to popularize the island as a vacation spot for residents of the mainland. Although a few resort hotels and other buildings were then put up on the shores of Avalon Bay near its southern tip, and an excursion steamer made daily trips from the town of Wilmington, little progress was made until 1919. In that year William Wrigley, Jr., heir to the Chicago chewing-gum fortune, secured large holdings in and about Avalon, built a $2,000,000 casino and numerous other improvements, and launched a nation-wide campaign to attract tourists. Thereafter the picturesque little community speedily became a favorite amusement center for thousands of Californians and others, and remains so to the present day.

Atop a high hill at the southern entrance to the bay Wrigley built an elaborate residence, modeled after an Italian palazzo, the windows and terraces of which command a sweeping view not only of the town and its boat-studded harbor, but, on clear days, of the mainland, some thirty miles distant.

One of the most interesting of California's literary shrines is El Alisal (The Sycamore), which stands at 200 East Avenue 43 in the Highland Park section of Los Angeles. Plainly visible from the heavily traveled Arroyo Seco Parkway, which connects Los Angeles with Pasadena and other towns lying to the east of the metropolis, this house — which has recently been made a State Historical Monument — was long the home of Charles Fletcher Lummis, who for a period of more than forty years devoted himself to spreading abroad a knowledge and appreciation of the attractions of that region.

Lummis himself was no less colorful than the area he delighted to describe. Born at Lyons, Massachusetts, in 1859, and educated at Harvard, he early developed an abiding interest in the primitive culture of the Southwest Indians, and for some years thereafter he lived among the various tribes, studying their history and customs and in many magazine articles and several books making his findings known to the world.

He first reached Los Angeles in the late 1880s, having traveled afoot and on horseback from Cincinnati — a distance of some 3,500 miles — and for a brief period served as city editor of one of the local newspapers. Routine journalism of that type was, however, not to his taste and we presently find him devoting his abundant energies to free-lance writing, to the publication of a booster magazine — first called *Land of Sunshine* and later *Out West* — and to the organization of a series of projects, among them the Sequoia League, the Landmarks Society, and the Southwest Museum, all designed to stimulate interest in the study and preservation of the region's outstanding features, both natural and man-made.

In the construction of his house, as in all things else, Lummis was never content to follow conventional procedures. Having, in 1894, selected a site on the west side of the Arroyo Seco — the most striking feature of which was a huge sycamore tree — he set about building it, mostly with his own hands, his only help being that of a group of Indian youths whom he imported from their ancestral pueblos in New Mexico, and who made camp on the spot throughout the construction period. The materials used were largely those that lay close at hand: its thick

95.　El Alisal, Los Angeles.　Long the home of Charles F.
Lummis, indefatigable writer and lecturer on the wonders of
the Southwest, this picturesque stone house was built, largely
with his own hands, in a grove of sycamores beside a stream
in the northeastern section of Los Angeles.　Upon Lummis's
death in 1928, he willed the property to the Southwest
Museum, of which he was one of the founders.　*Photograph
by Dave Packwood, Los Angeles*

walls of rounded rocks lugged up from the bed of the stream below, and much of the woodwork hand fashioned from trees that grew on or near the property.

Under the circumstances the big house, its main section two stories high, and with wings extending backward and enclosing his cherished sycamore tree, was a long time building. Even before its completion, however, it had become a favorite rendezvous for literary lights of the day, not only residents of the area but distinguished visitors from afar, for it used to be said that "You haven't seen Los Angeles until you've seen El Alisal."

Reflecting as it does the varied interests and enthusiasms of its owner, the structure conforms to no one architectural style, it being, in the words of one commentator, "a mixture, planned and improvised, of medieval castle, Indian pueblo and Spanish *casa*." Standing at one corner of the main building is the circular tower which Lummis used as a study, and where he frequently spent as many as twenty hours a day turning out the prodigious amount of material that over the years made him the foremost interpreter and popularizer of the romance of the Southwest, a veritable one-man Chamber of Commerce.

Upon his death in 1929, Lummis willed El Alisal to the Southwest Museum. Then, some fourteen years later, title to the property was transferred to the city of Los Angeles and it has ever since been maintained as a memorial to one of the most picturesque — and eloquent — of the area's early boosters.

PART

VI

THE TURN OF THE CENTURY, AND LATER

During the final decades of the last century and the beginning of the present, there were built in California a group of homes of a type that set new standards both in size and luxury.   The influences that brought these into being are well understood; their owners were merely following a national trend.   For the industrialization of the country in the years following the close of the Civil War had resulted in the assembling of many large fortunes, and this in turn had brought about the building of scores of impressive family homes on New York's Fifth Avenue, Chicago's Gold Coast, at Newport and Bar Harbor, and numerous other places from coast to coast.

Generally speaking, the mansions put up during that period were, in California as elsewhere, of a quite different type than those fancied by the rich men of preceding generations.   For the last-named had, for the most part, been self-made men, most of whom had sprung from humble beginnings and had been far too busy amassing their millions to have either time or inclination to develop standards of taste in the design or furnishing of their houses. By and large, they insisted only that these be big enough, and ornate enough, to serve as visible symbols of their success in accumulating impressive amounts of worldly goods.

When, however, in due course, these fortunes passed into the hands of the sons and daughters of their founders, this was no longer true. To those of succeeding generations the possession of great wealth was no longer a novelty; unlike their forebears, they had had the advantages of formal education, of foreign travel, and to some extent of acquaintance with the best in the art and architecture of their own and earlier periods. Hence when they came to plan homes of their own, few of them had any wish to duplicate the ornate Victorian structures in which they had spent their childhoods. Instead, they engaged the services of the most competent architects, designers, and interior decorators of their day and, having decided what sort of houses they wished, gave these specialists carte blanche to proceed.

Thus was ushered in what some commentators have termed California's golden age of domestic architecture, a period when there arose a group of mansions that in size, design, and in the elegance of their furnishing set standards unequaled either before or since. For they were products of an age that has passed into history, an age before the cost of maintaining such establishments, involving as they did the services of a small army of retainers — butlers, maids, cooks, gardeners, coachmen, and the like — grew beyond the means even of the wealthiest citizens. In the present more austere era, few of these showplaces dating from the turn of the century continue to serve their original purpose, the majority having been converted to other uses. Some have been torn down, others have long stood vacant, and still others have become resort hotels, private schools, clubs, and, in one instance, an art gallery.

Another significant development of that so-called golden age was a tendency to locate the great new residences, not in the cities themselves, but in their environs. Two factors were mainly responsible for that.

96.   The Uplands, San Mateo.   Designed by the talented San
Francisco architect, Willis Polk, this impressive neoclassic
residence has long been one of the showplaces of the
peninsula.   Built for C. Templeton Crocker, it is noted alike
for its interior finish of rare woods and marbles and for
its extensive formal gardens, part of which are shown above.
Photograph by Moulin Studios, San Francisco

First, the advent of the automobile and the building of adequate roads had made travel between home and office far more speedy and comfortable, and, second, by choosing a site in the country, the securing of enough space for the extensive grounds and formal gardens to set off the new structures properly presented no problem.

From the mid-1890s this movement into the surrounding countryside became increasingly evident, both in the Los Angeles and San Francisco areas. Throughout that period a number of wealthy San Franciscans chose to locate their new homes in the hills behind Oakland, Berkeley, and other towns on the east side of the bay, while others selected the picturesque wooded valleys of Marin County to the north of the metropolis and separated from it by the Golden Gate. A majority, however, elected to settle lower down on the peninsula on which the city itself stands, a decision influenced not only by the fact that the area abounded in attractive building sites but that it could be reached without the necessity of crossing the bay.

The result was that during this period there sprang up on the peninsula an impressive group of residences, built for the most part of stone, brick, or concrete, and in their design closely following European models of the best periods; namely, those of the French and Italian Renaissance, eighteenth century English manor houses, Spanish haciendas, and the picturesque villas of the Mediterranean coast. Today a score or more of these big houses are to be found there, most of them on elevated sites that command a view of the bay on one side and the high, wooded hills on the other, and set in the midst of parklike gardens many acres in extent.

Among the most notable of these are those of two members of the Crocker family, that of William H. Crocker, son of the railroad builder who founded the family fortune, and of William's nephew, Charles Templeton Crocker. The first, an Italian villa called New Place, was built in the early 1900s and stood in the midst of an estate comprising some 400 acres. The house was designed by Lewis P. Hobart, one of the leading architects of the period, and its formal Italian gardens were laid out by the renowned landscape artist, Bruce Porter. William H. Crocker was long an ardent collector of art objects and, having both taste and discrimination in such matters — as well as a bottomless purse — he over the years assembled at New Place a notable collection of European paintings, tapestries, bronzes, and statues. Templeton Crocker's The Uplands, nestled among the foothills near San Mateo, is an even more impressive residence than that of his uncle, being a huge, three-story structure of neoclassic design, the work of the highly gifted San Francsico architect, Willis Polk.

Another attractive peninsula estate is Montalvo, a handsome Italian villa that stands in the midst of broad lawns on a wooded hillside outside the town of Saratoga. Built by James D. Phelan, ex-mayor of San Francisco and later a United States Senator, it was named for a fifteenth century Spanish writer, Ordanez de Montalvo, in one of whose romances the name California first appeared. The approach to the villa is an impressive one, the driveway passing through entrance gates surmounted by stone griffins, winding upward between rows of Italian cypresses and Irish yews and coming out on formal gardens ornamented with pools, statuary groups, and graceful pergolas from which through the spring and summer each year depend long plumes of purple wistaria.

There Phelan entertained lavishly throughout his latter years. Having long been a patron of the artists, sculptors, musicians, and writers of the region, upon his death he presented the estate to the San Francisco Art Association for the use of promising students in these and allied fields. In recent years, however, the cost of maintaining so elaborate an establishment has proved beyond the resources of the association, and for the most part Montalvo has remained closed, with a single caretaker in charge.

Other impressive peninsula estates dating from the first decades of the present century are those of Joseph D. Grant and George A. Newhall,

233

97. Villa Montalvo, Saratoga. Standing on an eminence that commands a sweeping view of the Santa Clara Valley, and with the heavily wooded Los Gatos hills in the background, this was for many years the home of James D. Phelan, San Francisco capitalist and ardent patron of the arts. Upon his death he bequeathed his Montalvo estate to the San Francisco Art Association. *Photograph by Moulin Studios, San Francisco*

98.   Villa Rose, Burlingame.   So named because of the pinkish tint in which its outer walls are finished, this structure —
which has been termed "an unusually pure rendering of
Italian Renaissance architecture" — was long the country
home of San Francisco capitalist, Joseph D. Grant.   *Photograph by Moulin Studios, San Francisco*

both located in the town of Burlingame and both designed by Lewis P. Hobart who was responsible, too, for their handsome gardens. The first, known as Villa Rose, has long been admired as a choice example of Italian Renaissance architecture, while the second, built in the form of a Latin cross, is notable for its admirably proportioned façadès and for the extensive terraced gardens that surround it on all sides. These are but two of a score or more of such magnificent country homes tucked away on the hillsides and wooded canyons of the peninsula, nearly all of them put up during the early 1900s and for the most part still owned by descendants of their original builders.

Not all the noteworthy residences put up in the San Francisco district during that period were, however, located "down the peninsula." Long one of the showplaces of the region was the Hacienda del Pozo de Verona — The Estate of the Veronese Well — which stands on a hilltop overlooking the Livermore Valley, some thirty miles to the southeast of the metropolis, and which derives its name from the fact that an antique wellhead of Veronese sculpture once occupied the center of its patio.

From afar, this big, rambling structure, with its white walls, red-tiled roof, and lofty towers has the appearance of a Moorish village. Upon approaching nearer, however, the extensive gardens, the intricately wrought iron grillwork before its windows, and its ancient, massive doorways, reveal it as a re-creation on a truly magnificent scale of the sort of luxurious country seats fancied by the grandees of Renaissance Spain.

The hacienda was long the residence of Phoebe Apperson Hearst, widow of Senator George Hearst, millionaire mineowner, and mother of William Randolph Hearst. A woman of interests in many fields, she delighted to entertain on a grand scale. Frequently there were as many as forty weekend guests staying at the house, and few of the notables who passed through San Francisco in the early years of the present century failed to pay her a visit. Following Mrs. Hearst's death in

236

1919, the hacienda, like so many other big country estates, was converted to other uses. For by then the grandiose era that had created them was fast drawing to a close and the cost of maintaining such establishments was becoming burdensome even to their wealthy owners. During the years that followed, the Hearst property became first a stock farm for the breeding of thoroughbred horses, then a resort hotel, and finally a country club, which it remains today.

Nor was the building of such impressive residences — mansions was the term usually applied to them — confined to the San Francisco area. During that same period the southern half of the state saw the rise of numerous homes conceived and executed on a scale of similar magnificence. This was particularly true in and about Santa Barbara and in the eastern environs of Los Angeles, centering about Pasadena. For from about 1900 onward, wealthy men from other parts of the country, attracted both by the salubrious climate and the picturesque terrain of the southland, began taking up permanent residence there, with the result that Montecito, San Marino, La Jolla, and a number of other localities presently each had its group of luxurious estates.

One of the earliest — and most spectacular — of these is El Fureides (a name that, freely translated, means pleasure garden) which, surrounded by grounds more than thirty acres in extent, stands on an eminence in the Montecito Valley, with the lofty Santa Inez mountains on one side and the waters of the Santa Barbara Channel on the other. Built by J. M. Gillespie and known locally as "the Gillespie place," it is noted for the extent and diversity of its gardens — in which are to be seen more than 125 varieties of palms, together with numerous other rare trees and plants — and for the house itself. The latter is a great edifice that, in the words of one commentator, embodies in its design "elements . . . derived from Greece, from Rome, from Pompeii, from modern Italy, from Arabia and from Spain." The most striking feature of its plan is a series of terraced pools that form the main axis of the garden, each

99. Graham Villa, Montecito. Adjoining Santa Barbara
to the east and with its tree-covered hills overlooking the
waters of Santa Barbara Channel, is Montecito, long the
abode of a group of wealthy families whose estates border its
winding driveways. Above is shown the terrace of the former
Graham Villa, which stands on Eucalyptus Point and commands a view of Santa Cruz Island in the distance. *Photograph by Karl Obert, Santa Barbara*

pool lined with antique Spanish tiles and rising one above the other to the main façade of the house.

Another of the many handsome residences in the Montecito area is Arcady, an impressive Italian Renaissance structure designed by Russell Ray and long the home of George A. Knapp. This, too, is set in extensive gardens, replete with lawns and pools and fountains. The dominant architectural feature of the house is a graceful tower that soars high above the tiled roof and is visible from afar, rising well beyond the tall cypresses and other trees of its garden.

Fronting on the curving driveways of this so-called millionaire's colony are many other big estates, most of them screened from view behind high walls, and with the names of their original owners — among them Stetson, Armstrong, Pillsbury, and du Pont — reading like a roll call of the foremost business and industrial families in the nation. Among those that are deserving of mention, either for their architectural distinction, for the beauty of their setting, or for the magnificence of the furniture and art objects that have been assembled within their walls, three might be singled out. The first is known as the Roy Wilcox Estate, an imposing, wide-spreading structure suggestive of early Andalusia, the white walls and red tile roof of which blend harmoniously with the palms, banana trees, and other semitropical planting of its extensive gardens. Another is the Graham Estate, patterned after an Italian palazzo, which stands on a headland known as Eucalyptus Point, the windows and broad, tiled terraces of which command a view of the Santa Barbara Channel and of the group of islands in the distance. The third is the David Gray residence, in the spacious rooms and hallways of which has been gathered a truly remarkable collection of art objects: richly carved desks, tables, and mirrors dating from the 16th century and earlier, tapestries, candelabra, venerable statues of saints and virgins in wood and stone, and much else.

100. Roy Wilcox Estate, Montecito. Many of Montecito's handsome residences are patterned after those of Spain, their white walls, tile roofs and ornamental iron gratings before doors and windows being admirably set off by the semi-tropical vegetation of their extensive gardens. *Photograph by Karl Obert, Santa Barbara*

101. Grayholm, Santa Barbara. The former home of David Gray, this attractive residence, set in a grove of wide-spreading oaks, is an admirable example of how well the old casas of the Spanish and Mexican era can be adapted to present-day living. *Photograph by Karl Obert, Santa Barbara*

102. Hallway of Grayholm. Within, Grayholm is a veritable
museum of furniture, statuary, paintings, tapestries, and other
objects belonging to the best period of Andalusian art, all of
which are housed in an architectural setting appropriate to
their time.   *Photograph by Karl Obert, Santa Barbara*

PART VI: TURN OF THE CENTURY

Long one of the most widely known estates in the Pasadena area is that of Hulett C. Merritt, which stands within the city itself, fronting on Orange Grove Avenue and surrounded by formal gardens several acres in extent. The house, built of brick with an outer coating of stucco, has a number of features that attracted widespread interest at the time of its building. For not only its interior fittings but a great deal of its furniture was designed and made on the premises while the house itself was under construction. A variety of rare wood, much of it richly carved and arranged in intricate patterns, was employed on the walls and ceilings of the great main floor rooms. The entrance hall, which extends the full depth of the house, is finished in a pale mahogany, the drawing room in rosewood, the dining room in mahogany burl, while certain other chambers are paneled in tamaranga, a handsome hardwood that grows in the Andes.

In the summer of 1956, its owner having died, the furniture, paintings, and other *objets d'art* contained in the big, thirty-six-room mansion were sold at auction and the structure itself was offered for sale, yet another casualty of the nation's changing tastes in domestic architecture.

Long regarded as one of the most magnificent of California residences, and indeed having few equals anywhere on the continent, is the Henry E. Huntington mansion at San Marino, a few miles to the southeast of Pasadena. Built in the early 1900s by the wealthy landowner, transportation magnate, and collector of rare books, paintings, and objects of art, the great marble structure, designed by Myron Hunt, overlooks the San Gabriel Valley, with the rugged and lofty mountains of the same name rising in the background.

Surrounded by parklike grounds embracing more than 200 acres, the big edifice, together with its gardens, was long one of the primary interests of its owner, who devoted the final years of his life to its development, establishing there botanical gardens that for the variety and

103. Villa Merritt Olivier, Pasadena. Standing in a four-acre park near the center of Pasadena, this 36-room mansion, the home of the noted art collector Hulett C. Merritt, was long one of the showplaces of southern California. *Photograph by the A A A Photo Service, San Francisco*

rarity of their plants were unsurpassed elsewhere in the country, and acquiring scores of world-famous paintings to hang on the walls of his gallery. At the same time he bought en bloc virtually every important library that came on the market, thus assembling a collection of books and manuscripts that presently took rank with the most renowned in the nation.

Upon Huntington's death in 1927, both the mansion and the imposing structure he built close by to house his books, together with the many acres of gardens, were placed in charge of a self-perpetuating board of trustees, the residence becoming an art gallery and the adjacent building a library. Grounds and buildings are open to the public and daily draw throngs to view the gardens, to admire such paintings as Gainsborough's "Blue Boy" and Sir Joshua Reynolds' "The Tragic Muse" in the gallery, and the Gutenberg Bible and scores of other rarities on exhibition in the library. As has truly been said, Huntington's bequest of his estate and its treasures constitutes one of the most princely gifts of modern times.

Californians have long prided themselves on the fact that, when conditions warrant it, they are ever willing to strike out on new, untrodden paths. This, moreover, is one of their boasts for which there is considerable justification. For few unprejudiced observers of the behavior of the Native Son, from earliest times down to the present, will contend that an exaggerated respect for tradition has ever been one of his failings. There are sound reasons why this is so. The event that laid the foundations of the modern state was, of course, the Gold Rush, which took place a little more than a century ago. And it was the men drawn to these shores by that highly speculative enterprise who wielded the predominant influence during the decades that followed, and by nature these were nonconformers. The conservatives, the tradition-bound, remained prudently at home.

With men of that calibre holding places of responsibility throughout the state's formative years, it was not to be expected that they would be content to follow sedate, middle-of-the-road policies in either their private or public activities. Throughout California it was an age of experimentation, when the fact that a thing had never before been done in precisely that manner served, not as a deterring force, but as a challenge. Moreover, this attitute did not altogether die out with the passing of the pioneers. Something of their disrespect for tradition was carried over to succeeding generations, with results that are observable in many fields even today: in religion, in politics, and in certain aspects of social behavior. There is at least some justification for the boast sometimes made — usually by themselves — that Californians "make their own rules."

In view of that background it should surprise no one that the residents of the state presently began striking out on new paths in the design and furnishing of their homes. Indeed, the real cause for wonder is that they delayed so long before taking that perfectly logical step. During far the greater part of the period that has passed since the coming of the Forty-Niners, they and their descendants were seemingly content to live in houses closely patterned after their former homes both in Europe and in the eastern part of the United States, structures that, however well they may have been adapted to their purpose there, were suited neither to the California climate nor to the way of life of the residents.

The result was that not only did the settlements that sprang up the length of the Mother Lode, but the group of valley supply towns and the cities of the coast all exhibited so extraordinary a variety of architectural styles as to cause comment by numerous early-day journalists and others who have left behind a record of their impressions. One such, writing in the mid-1850s, stated that in strolling about the residential sections of any of the gold towns, one was likely to see "a New England farmhouse sandwiched between a prim Cotswold cottage and an elegant French chateau, while a bit farther down the street one comes on a Swiss chalet and, atop a neighboring hill, a white colonial

104. H. E. Huntington House, San Marino. This palatial, white marble residence, surrounded by handsome gardens many acres in extent, was built in the early 1900s by Henry E. Huntington, wealthy southern California landowner and transportation magnate. Today it houses the important collection of paintings and other art objects assembled by its owner during the latter years of his life. *Photograph from the Los Angeles Chamber of Commerce, Los Angeles*

manor house, complete with colonnaded façade, that might have been transported bodily from the Virginia countryside."

What is more, much the same course was followed throughout succeeding decades, the great majority of California residences put up during that period being based either on those with which their owners and builders had been familiar since childhood, or else being copies of the modes then popular in other parts of the country. The latter ranged from the austere clapboard dwellings with their pointed roofs and many-paned windows dating from Civil War days, on through the baroque flamboyance of the Victorian period to the extraordinary medley of styles and periods that characterized the domestic architecture of the state around the turn of the century.

Thus for decades California abounded in such outstanding examples of unfitness as — to cite but a few — dwellings with steep-pitched roofs standing in localities where snow had never been known to fall, of two- and three-story residences on ranches thousands of acres in area, and of prim, narrow-windowed structures occupying sites that commanded magnificent views. One extreme example of this blind following of tradition may be mentioned, although it concerns not a residence but a business building. Some years ago a firm of eastern architects was engaged to design a San Francisco skyscraper, and when the plans arrived it was discovered that provision had been made for the installation of steam pipes in the cornices, their purpose being to prevent the formation of icicles!

To be sure, there were a few hearty souls who, as early as the 1890s, revolted against the building of houses so ill adapted to local conditions and who proceeded to do something about it. These first tentative steps toward evolving a distinctly California type of domestic architecture consisted mainly of variations of the old adobe casas put up a century or more earlier by the Spanish and Mexican settlers. For these sturdy, thick-walled structures, while they possessed many features ill suited to modern living, nonetheless were in their design and treatment far more appropriate to their setting than the general run of houses built by the Yankees after California became an American state.

The reason for this is that over the greater part of California the climate is not unlike that of Spain, with warm summers, little rainfall, and an abundance of sunshine at all seasons of the year. It is a climate conducive to outdoor living, and the early adobes, both in the settlements and on the ranchos, were designed with that in mind, being for the most part single-story structures, virtually every room of which had doors opening to the outside. Moreover, the more pretentious of them were built in the form of a U, enclosing a central patio where the families spent much of their time, sheltered alike from observation and from such winds as might be blowing.

To be sure, these early adobes were by no means perfectly adapted to their settings. For while they were faithful copies of the rural casas of the Spanish homeland — and the climates of the two areas are, as stated, much alike — in the older country a levy known as a "window tax" was then in force, the result of which was that such openings were few and small. Hence the first California residences tended to shut out what has since come to be regarded as one of the state's major natural attractions; namely, its plenitude of sunshine.

When, around the turn of the present century, residences patterned after the old adobes — but with more liberal use of windows — began to be built, their advantages over most of the types then in use were quickly recognized, and it was not long before they were being widely copied from one end of the state to the other. This vogue for "mission style" houses, as they came to be called, lasted for several decades, during which many thousands of such structures were put up, ranging from great haciendas to modest four- or five-room cottages. Whatever their size or the degree of their authenticity, they had certain architectural features that made them readily recognizable: thick walls, tile roofs, and arched windows, with massive columns supporting their porches. While all were in imitation of the adobes, the majority were built, not of earthen bricks, but of wood, their exteriors covered with a veneer of plaster.

Although this long-continued era of "mission style" houses resulted in some highly attractive adaptations of the early Spanish and Mexican ranch houses, it was, taken as a whole, not one of the best periods of California domestic architecture. In recent times few of that type have been built and those still standing are regarded as definitely dated. However, when a new sort of distinctly California residence presently began to make its appearance, the houses embodied certain features of the old, notably the grouping of the rooms about a central courtyard.

Although the term "California ranch house" is frequently applied to present-day structures of this type, they are by no means confined to the rural areas. Throughout the central and southern parts of the state, and indeed everywhere save in the mountains and the extreme northern sectors, they have been built in steadily increasing numbers during the past quarter-century. Moreover, their growing popularity is easily explained. For more than any of their predecessors they embody features attuned both to the California climate and the California way of life. In size and cost and design they vary widely. All, however, are planned with the same end in view; that is, to render convenient the sort of outdoor-indoor existence that in recent years has become so characteristic a feature of California living.

This arrangement, which tends to make the outdoors a part of the living space, has brought about yet another change. Usually the houses are so laid out as to give them, not one but two garden frontages, one facing the street and the other in the rear, the latter often partially enclosed by one or two wings, thereby assuring not only privacy to those gathered there, but also protection from the winds that are frequent at certain seasons of the year. By this arrangement, virtually the entire lot, front and rear, can be attractively laid out with shrubbery, walks, and flower beds, and the cluttered, unsightly back yards of tradition are eliminated entirely, the service quarters being relegated to one side and screened from view.

Detailed consideration of the movement now under way looking toward the development of a distinctly California type of domestic architecture — and of the results thus far achieved — are, however, clearly outside the scope of this survey. For here the attempt has been made to present, both in illustrations and text, a picture of how Californians lived during successive stages of their region's evolution from remote Spanish province to complex modern commonwealth, a period that, in the brief span of less than two hundred years, has witnessed an admixture of diverse cultures and many racial strains that makes it unique among American states. Visible evidences of each phase of this remarkable transformation may be found on the preceding pages.

ACKNOWLEDGMENTS

For help in the compiling and writing of this book the author is indebted to numerous individuals and organizations. Those who supplied photographs used as illustrations are in each instance listed beneath the illustrations themselves. For assistance in the selection of what houses to include in this survey and, in many instances, for data concerning their historic or architectural significance, thanks are due to the secretaries of a number of chambers of commerce and other civic organizations from San Diego northward to the Oregon border, as well as librarians, county officials, and the managers and staffs of a group of historical societies, both local and state-wide in their scope.

Particularly useful has been the material supplied by the California Room of the State Library at Sacramento, the California Historical Society, San Francisco, the Bancroft Library, Berkeley, and, in the southern part of the state, the Los Angeles Chamber of Commerce, the Title Insurance and Trust Company, Los Angeles, and the Union Title and Trust Company, San Diego. Among individuals, grateful acknowledgment is made to the following: James Abajian, Harry W. Abrahams, Bettilee Byers, Florence Chessé, Carroll D. Hall, Phil Townsend Hanna, Norman Miner, Allan R. Ottley, Duncan H. Olmsted, and Caroline Wenzel.

INDEX

INDEX

INDEX

INDEX

INDEX

INDEX